APPLE'S DREAMS

A little girls' dream of becoming the President of the United States

APPLE'S DREAMS

*A little girls' dream of becoming
the President of the United States*

Kimberly Cécille Anicette

Copyright © 2020 Kimberly Cécille Anicette
ISBN: 978-1-7772906-0-3

A moment of silence for the little girl who had (almost) died on November 14th, 2017 from date rape drugs.

November 14th

November 14th, 2017,
You are a life lesson that our bodies are temples
And they should not be taken for granted.
The wrong touch could be a tiny ripple effect
That leads to the destruction of a life.

Contents

Chapter 1 | Apple - 1
Do not bite my Apple if it does not belong to you!
Ask first and you shall dig into my seeds

Chapter 2 | I had a dream - 29
A little girl dreaming of becoming
the President of the United States of America

Chapter 3 | Sunshine - 37
A little girl who lost her grandfather at the age of 6
as she got home from school

Chapter 4 | 523 - 51
Happy Birthday! What is your purpose little girl?

Chapter 5 | Canada Eh? - 65
We are going on vacation; to CAN-A-DUH!?

THE FUTURE IS Female, and that Female is Haitian. Vote Kimberly C. Anicette for President of the United States in the year of 2036! "***Kimberly's Combs***" is dedicated to you, the little girl with the apple barrettes; may your dreams come true, with all that you do.

About the Author

KIMBERLY CÉCILLE ANICETTE was born in Miami Florida, USA and raised in Niagara Falls, Ontario Canada. She is a brave, innovative, and ambitious young woman who dreams about becoming the President of the United States of America in the year of 2036. Kimberly Anicette enjoys ballet, poetry, singing, and music to distract herself from the biggest nightmare of Niagara Falls, Ontario. Her story will surprise and inspire many around the world, especially young girls and those who are trapped in the sex industry. Kimberly Anicette is an inventor who plans on creating amazing inventions as she believes her heart will change the world. Kimberly Anicette's nickname is "Apple" the forbidden fruit dedicated to the hair barrettes her mother dressed her in for her elementary school pictures as a little girl. Kimberly wants to redeem her power to light up the world with love and knowledge of how to successfully lead a nation.

*Certain words in this book are highlighted in **bolded***

italics *to reveal future businesses of Kimberly C. Anicette such as:*

Kimberly's Combs** | **Mon A Lisa's Pizza** | **Anicette liqueur** | **Higher Power** | **Save Haiti KC** | **The Kissing Booth** | **Sunny Booth** | **GUN to GUM** | **(L)OVE** | **Apples & Sunshine** | **Toilette de Anicette** | **Ghoti (pronounced as fish)** | **Plant It girl to Planet Girl** | **See my Eyes** | **CEO CTRs (stars)

Ben Vereen

The Iconic Entertainer

BEN VEREEN IS a famous entertainer, dancer, and actor with no relations to me pictured at the back cover of my book. At the age of seven years old he visited my ballet academy that I was accepted into which I had accidentally auditioned for at my school South Olive Elementary in Miami, Florida. I was waiting for my bus at the afterschool program I was enrolled in, sitting on stage in the cafeteria when a group of girls around my age surrounded me. The instructors began asking us to do the splits, turns, jumps, etc. and I was able to complete them all and got accepted the ballet academy. When I told my mother, she was surprised and was very happy because I was so talented, and the academy was free. I worked very hard to get the choreographies as correct as I could and would remember the steps quite quickly to stand out so my mother would be proud of me. Mr. Vereen came in one day with a feather earring, ankh necklace and a particular shirt, placed his hands on my neck and I was told to smile for the camera while looking at my reflection in the mirror. I aspire to be as great as Ben Vereen in the entertainment industry, where I want to excel in and leave a legacy. It would be an honour one day speak to Mr. Vereen about the photo we took at my ballet academy and who that little girl grew up to be.

Ben Vereen was the father of Will Smith in the Fresh Prince of Bel Air and in my opinion the best episode of the entire show. That episode explains exactly how those who grew up without a father's presence felt in their lives. When I look at the picture of Ben Vereen and I, I see a father figure who came to my ballet class and took a picture worth 1,000 words. Him standing behind me keeping my head up reminds me of a saying *"A man is the head and the woman is the neck, she keeps the balance while the man takes the lead"*. In the photo, his shirt is written with the saying "Billionaire in the making". How God placed Ben Vereen on my path to wear that exact shirt while meeting me for the very first time gives me the idea that I am able to be a billionaire. I will make it come true with this book in honour of the sequence of the day that Ben Vereen had woken up to have chosen that particular shirt, came to my ballet academy and take a picture with only me.

I was a ballerina whose air being my dance floor,

my choreography, my heart. The beauty in ballet and how important the air is when dancing heightens emotions, and I will give everything I have to reveal my story in this book as my "final dance". I will inspire little girls of colour to dance ballet and design wardrobes that compliment their skin tone in efforts to bring recognition to ballet dancers of all shades. Ballet was taken away from me because I moved to Canada in 2007 at the age of 8 years old. Ballet was the only time I was a happy child because ballet means freedom to me, you can express your feelings through motion of your body and release energy that is built in inside of you. With specific movements of your arms, legs, and posture you tell a story without a word and control your body to fulfill that story. I enjoyed ballet because I loved the experience of looking forward to dancing at the end of my school day and changing from my school clothes into my ballet attire without messing up my hair. I worked on becoming the best in the room and would often sneak away after class to watch the older ballerinas as an example of how I should dance. I was always a dancer, simply life did not agree with my dreams of continuing with ballet, I now must incorporate krump dancing to express my energy as an adult that the little girl inside of me has. My truth comes in the form of dance because that is the only time I am weightless physically and mentally where I can think about nothing but the music. I can listen to specific music given to me and my body will react like a spell that has lifted from me and I am myself again. My favourite music to dance to are love songs that resonate with my heart. Songs with different beats allow me to switch my tempo and demand attention to what my body and the little girl inside is trying to tell me.

Jeremiah 31:13
13 Then young women will dance and be glad,
young men and old as well.
I will turn their mourning into gladness;
I will give them comfort and joy instead of sorrow.

The bible says God will comfort those by removing their sorrow with dance when you return to him. I have given up the dance that was of the devil and became closer with the Lord. The Legend has brought me back to the Lord by helping me leave the darkness that consumed me. It was my choice to follow the light after being consumed with evil, because I found happiness in dancing how the Lord intended for me.

Chapter 1 | Apple

Do not bite my Apple if it does not belong to you! Ask first and you shall dig into my seeds.

I WAS A LITTLE girl who did not know what life would bring me to gift you. My mother clipped these apple barrettes in my hair, yet everyone said they were oranges. Due to my calming nature, I insisted over and over that they were, in fact pink, orange, yellow, green, blue, and purple, apples! In that sense, I was a very polished child with a crisp uniform on every day and only dressed in the newest button up shirt, pants, and shoes that my mother or I picked out for myself. I loved getting ready for school in the morning and feeling my mother's hands against my scalp with the brush. My hair, uniform, and shoes were the most important aspects about myself because it was a bonding moment with my mother. As a little girl my hair was a major part of my identity because it represented my mothers creativity and how the world judged me as an African American. Braiding was her technique for all of my hairstyles and her love for my silky hair made it easy to design with barrettes and earned me various compliments at school and everywhere I went. My hair texture was passed down from my maternal grandfather which gave her an immense pride for my genetics.

A comb is used to part hair into intricate sections and a very powerful symbol in the African American community in relevance for our afros. With my creativity I can design and plant forests by mapping out the trails firstly, through the most hated texture in the world. Kimberly's Combs will be a double meaning business to inspire African Americans to love their natural hair because our hair was once used as maps to freedom and hold deep secrets to our heritage. Kimberly's Combs will be a hair company in the world for not only cosmetics but for cancer patients, burn victims, and those suffering from alopecia or hair loss. From head to toe women and men will feel beautiful starting with the person they see looking back at them in the mirror. Beauty comes within but people judge our faces before they know our souls. Kimberly's Combs will empower those who feel their self worth is not valid because of the texture of their hair.

As a young girl I designed my clothes into pieces that

I thought were amusing but also necessary for my elementary school days. Pockets! There were never enough pockets on a pair of pants, so I drew out my idea of folded in boot cut legged jeans and put in extra crayons and other things I thought were important. I was very quick with my ideas and how to make them; creativity was all I was focused on from people to books, and money. I was always receiving inspiration from my surroundings especially the braille on the wall and elevator buttons, small dots read by those who are visually impaired. To me braille felt like regular bumps but to the intended person it made perfect sense for means of communication. Seeing braille as a young girl made me want to explore what people touch when they can't use their eyes and gave me a fear of ever losing my eyes. The apple of my eye was fashion, I created specific clothing for those who are visually impaired by placing diamonds on the openings of the fabric through my Higher Power clothing line. The significance of Higher Power is a double meaning of bringing light to the world by curing darkness. Light reflective and waterproof clothing signifies lighting up the world in countries that do no produce electricity such as Haiti and braille clothing signifies curing the darkness that blind people are accustomed to by incorporating it in fashion. The purpose is to have the car lights reflect on the clothing to promote pedestrian safety as well as supply raincoats, umbrellas, rainboots, etc. for the heavy rain that is prominent, often resulting to floods.

    CHRIMS are basketball shoes I designed for people with feet that have no soles which puts the pressure from their body onto their knees. The significance of

CHRIMS is to create a shoe line that dominates the footwear industry as there are unique feet with no soles and regular feet with soles. Complications can be developed due to the structure of a the foot and there are no shoes that mould soles gradually into the foot from infants to adults. The idea occurred to me because my favourite entertainer "The Legend" has flat feet who occasionally plays basketball, which prompted my acknowledgement on how many people are born with flat feet and how to prevent this from occurring. The athletic footwear industry is male dominated; therefore I would be the first female to have my own basketball shoe line as well as my own shoe foot pad with built in structure for those with unique feet.

My hair, clothes, and shoes meant very much to me as a little girl because I was accustomed to wearing a uniform. Apples were simply an image on my barrettes that was coordinated with my uniform as I went to school for knowledge. As I grew older, Apples became a significant factor in my life after puberty pertaining to sexual activity. The biggest controversy in life is Adam and Eve not the fact that they existed but who ate the apple. In my opinion Adam must have eaten the Apple and it got stuck in his throat. If Eve ate the apple, then how come females do not have an Adams apple? Very important questions. Is sex the forbidden fruit the bible is referring to or was it forbidden knowledge to making us think that we are Gods. Adam was created from dust and Eve was created from his rib. In my theory, if the apple represents sex rather than knowledge then once

Adam was eating the apple gaining wisdom Eve spoke the word that she was with child. If the apple represents knowledge rather than sex, then on the first bite Adam realized he was God himself and the garden as well as Eve belonged to him. There is only one Eve in this story and that Eve is me, I come from the rib of one man, no one else. The origin of Eve is the living and I am both the living and dead as a Zoe meaning zombie in creole. The biggest controversy in my day in age is consent when sex is involved. This Chapter is dedicated to consent and gaining knowledge of how predators can manipulate the act of consent by disregarding it or with the use of date rape drugs.

Sex is defined as the most satisfying action in the world. I wanted to remain a virgin until marriage, but teenage society pressured me into giving up my apple. I lost my virginity on February 3rd, 2016 at the age of 17 to someone I thought I would be with for the rest of my life and made me believe he was interested in my love. He invited me over to his house, I had gotten my nipples pierced because I wanted to feel and be sexy for him meanwhile, he led me to his basement couch. While we were about to "Netflix and chill" he put on Arnold S. working out at the gym which I kindly asked to switch the movie to Bad Boys 2 because it would made me feel more comfortable. My first time was not like I had imagined, could I go back in time I would never have lost my virginity at all but that's not how life works. I lost my virginity to the greatest movies on the planet starring Will Smith and Martin Lawrence! I think that is pretty epic because I had to stop and laugh at the Haitian scene, as it was my favourite part of the movie. For the ladies who have yet to experience such feeling- it hurts and is not pleasurable. If you want to wait until marriage, do so because now a days sex is as common as the $1 bill therefore why wouldn't you want to be a rare $2 bill that not a lot of people have touched. Sex can change a lot of things in your life and alter your self confidence. Your worth is not determined by the fact if a man wants to engage in intercourse with you because you are much better than that, much more beautiful than a simple ejaculation. This message is for my young sisters who have questions about sexual intercourse. Had I never lost my virginity, I would never have been desensitized by sex and became addicted to the feeling of having a man next to me even if he did not really care about me.

Rape Education

If you are a victim of rape, the first thing you need to do is get a rape kit performed on you at your nearest hospital before deciding on going to the police therefore you have documentation of the incident in your health records that cannot be disclosed to the public. What is a rape kit? A rape kit is a step by step procedure that is preformed by nurses on a rape victim, male or female to use as evidence in the court of law against your rapist. Rape is very difficult to prove therefore gathering as much DNA evidence as possible of the event will increase your chances of getting the justice you deserve.

10 things to know before a rape kit:

1. Do Not: Take a shower, clean the area, brush your hair, do not use the restroom or wash your hands, or alter anything on your body after the incident.

2. Get something to eat from your nearest fastfood restaurant such as: McDonald's, Wendy's, etc. and ask for a fresh paper bag if you feel you need to remove your clothes immediately because of the trauma.

3. Place your clothes that you had on during the incident in the PAPER bag DO NOT wash them or extra clothes to the hospital with you to change into after the incident if you plan on going straight to the hospital.

4. Bring your documentation forms such as your Health Card.

5. Take note of any injuries visible on your body that was a result to the incident.

6. Keep knowledge of your medical history to explain to the nurse

7. Take pictures of your visible injuries, your clothing, and of yourself to strengthen your case.

8. Be honest with the nurses and most importantly yourself about the incident. Do not block out any experience you faced because you are ashamed because you will not be judged at all.

9. You can stop, pause, or skip a step of the rape kit if you choose to, the rape kit is for your step towards healing no one will be mad if you decide to stop with the process.

10. Recover, meaning you will be given information to help you start your healing.

God keeps waking me up everyday which means I have not served his purpose yet.

When you do not want to be alive you simply just want the pain to stop so you find out ways to hurt yourself when you in fact end up hurting other people. I needed something quick and easy like turning the TV off. "Click"! In a snap of a finger I would meet my maker. See, consistent electricity is a luxury that most people dream of. Who am I to waste the power of God to be turned off? When I came into this world I was brought back to life with electricity to the heart. Before

I thought of my great plans, I had to become Apple. Apple is the fruit that was meant to grow in icy cold weathers for me to understand the value of sex.

It all started when my former best friend from high school was dumped by her boyfriend because he cheated on her at the end of her high school year in 2016. She told me about an ad online arrangement site she had been on to cope with being single. Men would pay her to go shopping and "not" have to do anything with them. I thought this was an amazing deal to get paid for doing nothing must be a dream (or a nightmare) come true. I tried my luck on the website to where I matched with a man instantly and we exchange phone numbers. He sent me a photo; I already had my photo on the website that is what targeted me to this man. His name is the Uncle, I met him after skipping class to drive to Toronto to get paid for doing nothing. Big mistake, I was about to meet the head trafficker without even knowing it. We met outside of his restaurant, he parked and once I approached his car, I realized he was not the man in the picture. He still got my trust by confirming it was him and that he was safe, I went in the car with him to his house tour. He told me about not working for free, meaning every job experience you get you must take something away from it and apply it to your real life. Those were not his exact words but at the time that is what I thought he meant. I was 18 when I first met the uncle, he was in his late 30s early 40s a tall black man heavy build around 200 pounds of pure lean fat.

He took me to his pool house and told me to unzip my pants, he only wanted me to show my pubic hair; So, I did. He asked nicely and told me he can get my hair lasered treated which would make it smooth like a baby while touching me inappropriately. He asked me what size underwear I wore and if I like thongs, he could buy me all the lingerie a girl can want. We became friends, or so I thought. He brought me inside his house and explained it was a $4 million property which I did not care for and he told me he can give me a massage with coconut oil, but he would not touch me inappropriately (but he did). I told him I had to go, and he gave me snacks for the ride home. He told me to kiss him goodbye when I said no I did not like kissing men, he was prominent on asking for a kiss after he drove me to my car and he gave me $100. That was the last time I saw him in 2016.

I never saw him again until October while I was in University where he would message me out of the blue moon to see how I was doing. He let me stay a night at his house but wanted to sleep in the same bed with me where I declined but forced himself onto the bed with me to cuddle. It made me uncomfortable, a $4 million house but his room did not suffice he had to sleep next to me, but where was I to go? He was holding me from behind therefore I just tried falling asleep. On my 19th birthday I met my pimp on a blind date which we were set up together by a high school acquaintance "the nephew" in the city and by the uncle but I did not know at the time of the relations to each other, I was naïve because he told me his uncle had been watching me which should have been a red flag alert. The pimp called me the next day without saying happy birthday with a deep mysterious voice and told me to meet him at the casino. My intuition tells me the casino was my first date option to see if I was of age for the ring. He was polite and bought me a drink, but I was already sort of high off of marijuana. I wore my heels, jeans, a blouse, and a jean jacket. The nephew knew I wanted a boyfriend from me telling him so, so I thought the pimp was interested in being my love. The pimp was bragging about his car being a Mercedes Benz, but I had my own car, a brand new Hyandai sonata that I had in my name. He told me to pack for the weekend and I did just that. He took me to his condo in Toronto to where I discovered that he had a girlfriend, excuse me, we had a girlfriend. I was never seen as a girlfriend to a man before, therefore, to be a "girlfriend" to a man and woman I thought that was flattering. The nurse was her name she was blonde, 27 and jealous of a black girl who would be taking her place. The nurse was my second pimp while studying for nursing school, to think? she would go to school come home to a kidnapped girl in her house that she secretly despised. I was not allowed to go home nor go to work after the weekend and would have to call in sick while the pimp took my car.

The nurse took me shopping to show me how great her lifestyle was. She told me about Indian suitors who would pay us $1500 simply to go to Caribana with them and have fun. She brought me to my first Gucci store purchasing an $800 pair of jean pants. She wanted to show off her money, but money did not make me happy I was searching for love. She brought me home and got ready for work she showed me her shoes they were 8 inches in height, I was confused on how you were supposed to work in shoes like that. The pimp brought me to multiple dance clubs in my car for me to go ask if I could work that night. Being a black girl is not as easy asking for a job at the club, yet I finally got one at the landing strip next to the airport. The nurse would come to pick me up from work and bond with me like a girlfriend with friend tendencies. She would cat call guys and flirt with them in front of me which trained me to think that that was OK when it was absolutely not. She bonded with me in such a way like she wanted to tell me what I would be experiencing as a stripper but chose not to because I was taking her man away from her.

The pimp brought me to Windsor to a strip club with his friend Triple T and his girlfriend, who asked me to send her my pictures because the owner had to first approve, then you would be accepted to dance. Triple T was more of a man than my pimp was, he was protective and caring to me like a daughter. While I was there the first night, I made $800 and did not have to engage in intercourse with the clients at this club as it was not allowed. I was very proud of myself and thought that I could do it all over again for the money and thrill but as soon as we got back to the hotel, he took it all. The next night I made $300 which was incomparable from the $800 I made the night before, but he did not say anything he was nice about it and again took all the money. I had an altercation with another pimp because I bumped into him he almost shot my face off because he was so mad at me and my pimp came into the altercation and rescued me, THAT is when I developed strong feelings for him. The altercation started when a dancers' friend thought that I was trying to take her client when the client was asking for me which I told him to wait because I had promised other clients that asked for a dance that I would come back and give them the dance that they had asked for.

The 10 ho Commandments for the strip club

1. Get your money upfront

2. Keep count of your songs

3. Do not talk to another person's client

4. Wait your turn to wow the client if they rejected the previous dancer

5. The stage is your virtual sales pitch

6. Stay classy but nasty

7. Always carry a baby wipes and extra bandannas

8. Do not take any drugs offered to you

9. Do not go back to the client's house

10. Do not drink on the job, drink water, and pretend it is tequila. If the club does not allow this, then do not work for them because they do not care about your safety.

The next night I would make zero dollars; I tried my best but my soul was just not feeling it because the night before my pimp had told me how easy it would be to get kidnapped put in the back of the trunk and no one would ever see me again because of the altercation, which scared me very much. Triple T carried a concealed gun around his waist, a baby Glock for protection for his girlfriend and himself since someone snatched his chain, but I never saw my pimp with any weapons to protect me. We went home and that is when everything would soon change. We brought the benz back, but I did not know that the nurse was driving my car to work as she did not ask me for permission. Fast forward a week later she had called the police and told them I had stolen her Benz CLS 550, a $200,000 car she paid $15,000 for. I was acquitted because I did not steal her car, she took her information such as her insurance and ownership out of the car to set me up which is defamation of character since I was wrongfully convicted because I was black. That is a 10-year sentence in jail had I been charged with grand theft auto.

Previous to the nurse claiming I stole her car and last time I saw her she forgot $1200 in my glove department when the pimp took me 3 hours away to Windsor to work. I drove back to Toronto to give it back to her because I frequently travelled across the New York and Canadian boarder and did not want to be asked why I had a Caucasian woman's wallet in my car with extensive amounts of cash. She thought I would steal it but I had no care in the world for her money, I complied with everything the nurse and the pimp told me, looking back I was overcome with fear. When the nurse put in a claim that I stole her car it really messed me up because I had proven to her that I was not a thief and she called me the next day on an unknown number screaming at me that I was seen driving her car and other ridiculous things.

Before she put in the claim that I stole her car, I knew that the pimp was still seeing a girl because I found lip stick in the car when him and I were the only ones driving it. Once I confronted him about the situation, he told me that I should not question him and other emotionally and mentally abusive statements that were assertive and dominant which made me sad. He told me to go to Triple T's house and wait for him to arrive which ended up being a big mistake. As I pulled up to the house, I said to myself "something is going to happen to this house". The pimps brother later had come and shot at the door where I was walking past, there was a two second difference between me getting my leg sprayed with about 60 small pallets of bullets. I have never experienced such trauma of a gun shot that it went through the door onto the closet past the wall I did not know what to do but laugh. I thought it was a joke until I realized it was serious since all three of us were hiding upstairs and was oblivious to how serious the situation was. In the song Yellow tape, The Legend says: "You know your killers they fear my nigga"; I experienced this at that moment this is why I was laughing because I was the actual gangster in the room laughing after almost being shot, but I most definitely would have lost my legs and possibly could've died that night. The pimp was very calm about the situation and was partying that night with his cousin. He told me to keep quiet about the situation and failed to ask if I was ok

What type of girl was I in the club? I was shy and quiet but on the dance floor I was the best one to perform. I did so well because it was similar to dancing ballet that I missed the opportunity when I moved to Canada. My sales pitch was that I was the fresh meat, the youngest in the crowd with the lowest mileage and I was cute ending with my irresistible smile demanding to be looked into my eyes to gain control. I kept a baseball hat on so the men would automatically see me if I would stand next to anyone else, I made that my signature accessory. I danced to very provocative songs and knew how to work my body around the pole like a snake or ballerina. I spoke to every single client as opposed to most girls who let the clients come to them and just sat at the bar the whole night texting. I did not care if I got rejected, I would try again. I was very fair, and I did not scam my clients because my reputation and safety meant more to me than money and I thought it was a fun job being able to dance and listen to music all night. If I got rejected, I would quickly get up and leave and ask to perform on stage to bring out my best moves and would attempt to change their minds to take me for a dance. I would often ask the client to play pool if he did not want to dance to "make time go by" and would bet that if he lost, he would take me for one dance. I pretended I did not know how to play pool at first until he got comfortable and then I smoked him (I knew how to play because I was taught the game when I was 8 years old) bingo! Now I know that once I get him to the back, he will want more dances.

The music I danced to frequently was hip hop, and songs with explicit literal meanings. Whenever I wanted to dance to the song Questions I would be denied because it was "too short" but really it was because I was black since they let the white dancers dance to the Legend's songs, including Questions which is two minutes and the required time was three minutes. I began getting jealous and was developing interest for "The Legend" through his voice. I told myself I did not care about The Legend therefore I continued with my solid three tracks where I could be sensual and sexy with each lyric in the song. I definitely gave an impression on everyone but if I got rejected it was because I was black, they were too cheap, or they were regulars too deep in the game. All the girls danced to The Legend's music especially when Heartbreak On A Full Moon was released, I began finding myself distracted when I was working because every time someone put his song on I had to look to see who it was and if they were better than me. His songs would constantly play, and it was getting very annoying because all I could think about was his picture in my desk as a little girl, so I went out and bought his album. I discovered that his song Emotions says my name Kimberly at 0:28 seconds. I would then go on to change my songs to love songs such as T-Shirt by Destiny's Child and got lost in my inner emotions, all eyes were on me when I was performing, even the girls that hated me, hated me because I was too good. My pimp never saw me perform.

I met my rapist at the club after one of the best performances I ever performed, that kills me that my show made him automatically want to have sexual intercourse with me. He was the first person that I saw and made my way over to, literally out of breath but in the room full of people our eyes locked. He was Caucasian with dark features and blue eyes, not my type but attractive until you got close up. I would sometimes wear my glasses to see my clients better and decipher the crowd, giving me a nerdy look. He sparked conversation with me without even any effort and the first thing he asked me if I was the owner of the CLS 550 outside I said no it belong to my friend. He talked to me about how he could help me leave the club and got my excitement because I told him I did not want to work in the club anymore and wanted to get into real estate to which he promised to help me.

November 14th

I went out to dinner with the rapist and he chose the location in St. Catharine's, 15 minutes away from my hometown. I was wearing a white dress with a bee necklace with my hair slicked up in a bun I went to the bathroom to take pictures to send to my pimp while he was waiting for me at the dinner table for about 15 minutes. I was also on my period, he bought me tampons that night from the shoppers drug mart because I had none left and did not want to result in using a sponge. He was mad at me that I would make him late for buying me tampons. That sure gave him the impression that I did not want to be there nor have sex and when he arrived, he was wearing a wrinkly gym shirt, jeans, and dirty running shoes while I was elegant and was rushing me into the restaurant. I bought him shoes and a birthday card to which he did not care about because he lied it was not his birthday; he just wanted to have sex with me that night. He intentionally chose the restaurant next to a hotel so he could make up a scenario that I was a prostitute wanting to have sex with him for money with consent. LIES!!!!! He told me he was tired, and I shouldn't drink and drive so we could head back to the hotel room where he would bring me my stuffed teddy bear, he had "bought" me, snacks, and tequila. Once he came back to the room I went to take a shower to go to sleep he came into the shower with me with 2 cups already poured with tequila I drank from the cup and felt nothing he told me to drink some more and kept pouring me about six shots on top of the four I already had at dinner. For me once I start drinking tequila I get drunk quickly because I don't drink alcohol I do not indulge because I know I cannot handle myself and I do not like the feeling of being drunk because then you are not aware of your actions. He wanted to touch me in the shower, so I got out of the shower and onto the main room where I looked at the microwave clock saying "9:11pm". He pushed me onto the bed and started giving me oral sex without my consent I definitely did not say yes to that, I was so drunk that all I could do was laugh but my mind was saying no. He brought out a condom and climbed on top of me inserted himself inside me to which he pulled out a few seconds later with blood everywhere it looked like a homicide. I snapped out of my drunken state and knew something was wrong by then it was too late I started throwing up and I dozed off. He went to the bathroom to clean off the blood on him because he had taken my tampon out. That is the last thing I remember is hearing the sound of the sink running. I woke up the next day 11 hours later, I was "dead" for 11 hours while he touched me and did God knows what to my body like a corpse. He violated my privacy, my womanhood, my dignity, and my vagina that did not belong to him. The thing that haunts me is that I do not know if he filmed me for his sick twisted fantasies that were not realistic so he had to rape me because I laughed that he could not perform and would not leave my pimp for him. I asked him what happened the night before I thought I just fell asleep I did not remember anything yet. The night before lasted about 5 minutes honestly, from the shower to the bed before I blacked out. I woke up he was already up, next to me staring at me so I began to talk to him for maybe a couple minutes and he asked me if I wanted to have intercourse to which he brought out cherry lubricant. Ugh I hate the artificial smell of cherries; it will make me feel sick and have a panic attack but real cherries I can tie the stem in my mouth! I asked him why he had that opened already and he brushed it off. I said I didn't want to have intercourse and went back to sleep because I told him my stomach was really hurting me. I woke up and remembered a small part of what had happened so I asked him about it but I was so naïve I did not understand what he had just did because in my mind I would not allow that thought because I was so strong it would never happen to me because I knew better. The year before on November 14th 2016, I was almost raped in a mans condo the night after the biggest UFC fight and the Harley Quinn character movie came out with the joker, but I escaped and the man got charged with assault even though he was groping me so hard my pelvis cracked and his hair from his stubble beard was all over my clothes because I wouldn't have sex with him. The rapist knew what he was doing since I shared my story with him before. The rapist told me that his family was from Belgium and what they used to do to African slaves. He told me that they would chop their bodies up such as their hands their arms and hide their bodies. To this day I do not know why he felt the need to bring that up other than the fact of to bring upon fear into me. I asked him what happened the night before he would not tell me. He told me that he was going to get me a joint from my car since I was asking so many questions but now, I realize that he was going to get more drugs and try to rape me again. I was asking too many questions therefore he took out his phone and started recording me onto his voicemail to which I did not care because I wanted to know what did he do to my body I said it's OK I forgive him just let me know and I won't get mad and he kept lying to me all I could think about was how, how, how, and why. I got my things and left to go to my car to go home but I was so distressed I could not drive I almost got into an accident. I had to call my younger friend to ask her what she thought could have happened to me and she was confused as well.

Kimberly Anicette's diary entry November 15th, 2017

Guess what fucking day it is. Guess what fucking happened to me. So, the rapist is a new man in my life which

I have only known for four months. This guy says he's got so much money and always asks me if I want to make money. Well this dumb ass got me drunk and fucking raped me. I still can't fucking believe this happened to me ON NOVEMBER 14th, AGAIN. That's fucked, the fuck up, I still can't believe it. I've been sexually assaulted and now rape I can't even think usually my brain is into reality, but right now I don't know what to do. I don't know what he is capable of because he says that he worked in private investigation. I think he prays on young girls (black ones probably) And those who are vulnerable. Or maybe this is his first offence LOL Fuck that this guy is A liar and wants shit from girls but is a predator he was telling me all this shit to do to November 14, 2016 and all of a sudden, he does this? Come on. He knew what he was doing I want to see what the drug results say because if he drug me that's even more fucked because I believe November 14, 2016 was going to drug me but anyways this man is not going to get away with it and I will take him for all his money I think this was supposed to happen to me as much as it sucks, I have to except it. Boy I can't and I don't want to right now this is fucked up I can't trust anybody. NO ONE. Men are all dead to me, men are fucking pigs and I'll meet someone who loves me, who actually loves me I am so fucking upset.

    A few weeks later I had called him disgusted and was verbally accusing him of raping me which he was laughing and told me he did not have to worry about me anymore. HE said that I told him in the restaurant that I wanted to have intercourse with him, and we had conversations of getting a hotel together to spend the night. I told him I never said I wanted to have sex with him and the hotel he was speaking of was a different location which was a spa. He had taken me to a spa before and I fell asleep through the whole massage with no recollection of any of the massage the woman told me I fell asleep and never moved.

After I was raped, I told the pimp to which he did not believe me, he said I was conscious for it all and wanted it. After this I went back to work and worked harder than I ever did, nonstop because I wanted to prove to him that I was telling the truth through being consistent.

How did I leave the club? On my hour and a half drive home at 2AM I would play The Legend's songs to disconnect with the club, since I was not allowed to dance to his songs. I loved the song Questions and Yellow tape the most because Yellow tape is a prayer for help, I understood every line in his song because I was stuck in a situation I could not get out of. Heart Break on A Full Moon became my therapy and was detaching me from the club into reality that everyone who has a normal life lives but now I was stuck in between two worlds that I felt like I didn't belong in either. I would feel something in me to not go back inside the club certain days due to an immense feeling of danger. There was a girl named "Cinderella" who was stabbed and left for dead because of money and an altercation that had happened in the club she worked at previously.

I wanted to tell the police everything I was dealing with, but my mom came to pick me up just in time for my siblings Christmas recital. Once I got home, I got ready putting on a white dress exclaiming how I wanted to get married with my hair a mess as I had no time to fix it, my depression and anxiety altered what my reality was as I was not prepared to come back to the real world without letting go of my pimp because I had done too much for him.

The lyrics of The Legend songs made me re-evaluate my life decisions to be a stripper working for my pimp. Life had not seemed real after eight months of being in the dark hole because that lifestyle is not real. Yellow tape made me realize that my pimp did not care if I died, let alone if I gotten raped it was just about the money. Heartbreak on A Full Moon planted flowers in my mind when I was in the darkest state of mind. No exit, for example the only route to take if you want to exit is to the jail cell or the coffin.

I will plant flowers in minds throughout the world with my help Plant It Girl to Planet Girl will be my foundation planting flowers, trees and food for the homeless every city that I tour in with The Legend. Being signed to OHB will give me the opportunity to plant flowers in the mind of someone else who is homeless who feels there is no exit as well as no entry for them to live on this world. Eventually homelessness will be cured as Higher Power and black pyramid will cure the disease that people must suffer in this world because that is not true.

I will give people the platform to do great and get an education to plant success into this world that children will be inspired to grow up in and create a better future for the next generations to come. Many people in this world wish to have an abundance of money. They think that will solve ALL of their problems, well I am here to help solve that problem by offering 1 Million to those who email (applesdreamskc@gmail.com) about a serious business plan and/or patent they wish to come into fruition and follow the Instagram page @apples_dreams. The great wall of CEOs will be in alphabetical order displaying your company and its purpose. The world will see your work ethic as well as your desire to become rich. I have created hundreds of inventions for my patent company but what is the use of being filthy rich if I cannot help others fulfill their true destiny and help me change the world? CEO CTRs will be my legacy to help families gain generational wealth and change the way this world functions around money.

Bel La Vie with Kimberly Anicette

Reading the book 15 years and 14 Chapters by Natalie Watson has changed my life drastically by shifting my mindset from my experiences. She helped me believe that I was not a weak person through her five points on fear:

1. Self Sabotage

No negative talk to yourself

2. Comfort Zone

Step out of your comfort zone

3. Mindset

Changing your mindset from negative to positive

4. Transparency

Be transparent with yourself and with others and see how your life changes

5. Manage Fear

Fear does not exist as it is a question of "what if", fear is the opposite of faith which is believing "even if"

Bel La Vie with Kimberly Anicette will be my self publishing book company and YouTube channel to give a platform to the voices of those who are slaves of sex without their consent or any personal life story that has been destructive to your well being. Most people believe that holding their pain within will help heal them, when speaking up is what starts the process of healing within. Like an appointment with a therapist, journaling and letting go of your pain will be the life changing experience you never thought you needed. I will have my own book club and hand out gold star and thunderbolt pins for positive reinforcement that you are made from stardust and are as excellent as the galaxies up above.

Trafficking Tip One: Location

Traffickers will relocate you from your family and friends to keep control over you. Cities divided by boarders are key hot spots for traffickers to recruit vulnerable women and as well as traffic drugs through out the country. Researching your community history will keep you aware of the dangers that lay in front of the naked eye. Always keep your surroundings in mind if you plan to make an exit, such as tourist attractions and hospitals are recommended.

Chapter 2 | I had a dream

A little girl dreaming of becoming the President of the United States of America

Work by Q Money | I don't die by Joyner Lucas and Chris Brown

THIS IS MY anthem for you. I am a "zoe" meaning bone or "zombie", saved by the spirits since before I was born. I am of the original zombies that were copied for the white man's storytelling. I am a real-life angel and "zombie" to protect the Earth, my Haitians will be saved, and the land will be protected through strong prayers, I will make sure of it. My creole runs deep in my blood and will run deep in your roots as well. All you have to do is be faithful in God and we will change the world together. Listen to the lyrics carefully and understand how they relate to *my* purpose in *your* life. I am Kimberly Anicette for a purpose, I will go down in history as a legend in life and death. I will go to war for my people and sacrifice my life to leave a legacy behind of prosperity and change.

Toussaint Louverture was a Haitian general who led the first slave revolt in the history of slavery in Haiti by emancipating the slaves on the land and conversing to the French generals to let them pave the way to their freedom. His infamous line "*Cut their throats and burn their houses*" would go down in history for killing Caucasians who owned slaves and Mullatos who were a product of rape.

I want to lead a nation with my voice as well as by listening to the voices of the people who vote for me. Natural born leaders intuitively posses the correct attitude to be in command, and I believe you must be born a leader.

The most successful way to reach and influence millions of people around the world is through music, captivating your listeners with your lyrics. My voice is my power, it sets me apart from 7 billion people in the world. My words are powerful enough to make changes in the world because I believe my words are art on a canvas that will be showcased globally, this book is my butterfly effect. Becoming a musician has been my dream because it is the first step to bringing me serious opportunities to be a leader in the Haitian and American community by permanently setting an example for generations to come using my voice. Popularity of the rich and famous influence our world heavily, the President is the most popular person in the United States who influences how Americans live. As I am writing this book it is the year of 2020, at the age of twenty two years old in Canada. I have fifteen years until I am eligible to run for the Presidential elections which should be held in the year of 2036. This means I have 15 years to get to work on strengthening my voice through my actions by aiding those who have no chance of the opportunities those in America have. If I can successfully create a plan to help people in poverty stricken countries, I can use those tactics to change the lives of Americans with a greater impact. Creating a system that promotes individual growth will benefit the whole country by focusing on finding solutions to the most prominent problems. Eradicating poverty and supplying education is the most important aspect to changing the way a country evolves. As a little girl I was advocating for the people in Haiti who had been affected by the Earthquake and left with absolutely nothing.

Email to my local newspaper editor

From: Kim Anicette
Sent: January 27, 2020 12:44 AM
To: B.C.

Subject: Re: Kimberly from STARBUCKS

The article "one small school makes a big effort for Haiti" was published ten years ago at my elementary school. Now that we are in a new decade that I call the Roaring 20's and I am 21, I started a non-profit and profit foundation to support Haiti "Apples and Sunshine" which will focus on feeding the hungry, specifically children with roaring tummies. I hope to accomplish building a school in Haiti and develop a feeding program in exchange for the attendance of the students. I have created businesses to support my efforts to ignite the land of Haiti.

The Kissing Booth is a business partnered with the Apples and Sunshine foundation because apples take after the shape of a single heart and the start of digestion starts with the mouth, me wanting to feed the hungry stems from love. My favorite subject in high school taught by my biology teacher Mrs. Booth was the digestive system she impacted me so much that I want to own a brand that supplies the less fortunate with access to healthy oral hygiene.

1. *Teeth -* ***The Kissing Booth***

2. *Throat -* ***My voice***

3. *Stomach –* ***Apples & Sunshine***

4. *Toilettries –* ***Toilette de Anicette***

Locally, I plan on distributing care packages on Valentine's day to local shelters from socks, underwear, toothpaste, and toothbrushes, hopefully, my acts spark love in the hearts of those who need it the most. I moved to Canada in February of 2007 living in shelters myself and this is will be my second decade accomplishing my life's purpose and making an impact in Canada.

"Small school makes a big difference for Haiti Kim Anicette" News Article

The earthquake that devastated Haiti hit close to home for me, Kim Anicette. As an 11-year-old Niagara Falls girl I lost a family member in the disaster and my home wall was destroyed. I asked the St. Joseph Catholic elementary school principle if they wanted to help reach out to my family and others in the small island nation. *"I know I'm very lucky to be here in Canada, because I have food and I have a shelter"* I said. *"In Haiti they have nothing and I wanted to help"* I led a prayer service at my school and asked teachers and students to contribute to my Haiti relief fund which the students asked their parents for donations and ransacked their piggy banks. Pennies, dimes, and dollars came pouring in. Fewer than five days we had collected $550 which was quite a remarkable situation in Saint Joseph's since we only had 130 students. My principal is the reason why I am who I am today. Mr. L believed in me and decided to let me have my own fundraiser. He is the reason my voice is loud and powerful simply because one day I asked Mr. L is it possible to raise money for Haiti since the earthquake happened, he said yes. With no hesitation he believed in my spirit, for that I'm forever grateful. It's because of teachers and principals like Mr. L that form a greater world more than they can ever imagine. Mr. L only knew me as a skinny little girl who could throw a football cross the field but once he met me and spoke to me, he knew my purpose was much greater. In 2009 my life had changed forever for the whole world to see. No one cared about Haiti before they saw opportunity to make money from the earthquake. The Red Cross raised $500 million in donations for the earthquake relief promising to build homes but only six were built. My purpose stems from this moment as I was a little girl who impacted more lives than they did as a major organization.

There are two types of people in this world those who want to eat in those who want money. When the world realizes you cannot eat money some will eat each other, others will eat the earth. No trees, no air, means no life on Earth. Deforestation will be prominent throughout the world globally causing the earth to look like a water planet. CTR (star) CEO, I was meant to be my own boss Mr. L had an eye for things like that, he knew which student was a good apple and which was a bad apple. I believe he knew I was a mix of both, without him there would be no *one small school makes a big difference for Haiti*. Thank you, Mr. L for bringing out the greatness in me hiring me for my first job at 10 years old by giving me access to the fountain of life and great purpose.

Dear Barbados and CARICOM,

As the future President of the United States of America I would be honoured to declare my services to your country in return for unity with Haiti. All Haitians stranded on your island with the promise of successful paying jobs shall be relocated to their proper home where they do not need Visa's on their birthright land. CARICOM is a Caribbean community organization of fifteen nations to promote cooperation of goods, services, persons, capital, and technology. I will save the land of Haiti by transforming the land into the most prosperous nation in the Caribbean that it once was. I am offering labour work and temporary living for Barbadians and CARICOM associated communities who want to aid in the rebuilding in the beautiful land of the mountains with the exception of women and children. My reasoning is to strengthen the CARICOM relationship with Haiti that will be an example to the world of how I, Kimberly Anicette will transform the Caribbean Community into a multi profitable organization partnered with my personal foundation **Apples & Sunshine.** I shall be a noble woman to all fifteen Caribbean islands associated with the CARICOM to demonstrate how I will unite the remainder of the world promoting peace and unity when I become eligible to run for President of the

United States in 2036. With my status I will provide your country with necessities for women and children such as paid labour work and tools for proper education through the CARICOM. It would be my honour to uplift Barbados and the fourteen other Caribbean Islands associated with CARICOM to benefit the future generations to come with what Haitians live on daily: Hope. The hope I have to offer comes in the form of architectural structures in Haiti that will transform lives through emergency response and of course, education. This is a once in my lifetime deal that will expire in the year of 2023 due to the injustices Haitians have faced on being rejected by your politicians. The Haitian passport shall be the most demanded and difficult passport in the Caribbean community to obtain because we are the first black led republic in the world, the most prosperous island in the Caribbean.

Sincerely,

Kimberly Anicette, the future President of the United States of America

Dear Haiti,

My fellow Haitians! I know times have been difficult for you, but the darkest hour is just before dawn. My ancestors saved me in order to save you therefore you should learn my name now, before we get to work on developing our country. This book will tell you everything you need to know about me and how I will save Haiti during what I call the Roaring 20's. I will fill your belly and your minds if you fill my soul with immense happiness and safe prayers to continue my God's work to bring peace to the world. Our language Creole will be universally known but not understood to the white man because they will destroy us and everything I am working hard towards. Remember how they treated us; our land will be the prosperous black led republic it always was with my innovative talents to bring our bloodline to the end of time. The men will rebuild the nation and the women and children will be educated to gain strong minds for the war that is about to take place. We are the originators of the slave trade, Africa runs deep in our blood, the white man has cursed us with illnesses, poverty, and lies that made us believe we are nothing but apes that have evolved in the flesh! We are the superiors of the Caribbean nations because Hispaniola was the first and most important slave port and the others have the audacity to disown us because of a mere boat stop that brainwashed them into thinking we are different. We are superiors! We will eat! We will prosper! For our children deserve to eat Apples instead of the dirt that is cursed with the white man's debt. Our work will be silent and irrelevant to the world until it is too late for them to listen. I hear your tummies rumbling all the way in Canada. I first heard it in 2010 when I was a little girl! It has been time to aid my people with what we were robbed of! The Red Cross stole our money for their rich lifestyles and gave us no hope for the future. I will rebuild this nation with my hands as this is what I am doing as I write this book. I am the angriest child that wants CHANGE. I am Kimberly Anicette, if you do not protect me now, I will come back in the next life and demand the peace I am asking for because I am tired of seeing my people suffer. I am tired of being denied access to my country because of the dangerous conditions that the children are screaming to me that will not go away. I am the Kimberly Anicette that will destroy THE PAIN OF HUNGER! I am the Kimberly Anicette who will bring solar energy and control it with the hands of Haitians. I am the Kimberly Anicette who will control the winds that fill my lungs. I am the Kimberly Anicette who will "eat" the dirt so there is nothing left but proper soil to plant fruit and vegetables. I am Kimberly Anicette, I am hungry and when I get hungry, I will eat everything in my path. My fellow Haitians, the time is coming, matter fact it has passed 10 years ago as I was disguised as a small little girl who had to watch on the television that underneath the Earth brought chaos. THE CHILDREN will not suffer anymore, not on my watch. THE CHILDREN will have their voices heard because they are the Gods of our universe. THE CHILDREN will be educated into intelligent Einstein's that will continue the marathon for peace if my life is prematurely taken when I am President. My fellow Haitians! We are the strongest army in the world without the need of protection because our skin is resilient. My fellow Haitians listen to this prayer and protect me as I will be the

Alpha wolf who will oversee everything the white man wants to destroy us with. My fellow Haitians I am here; I am sorry it took me ten years, but I am here. I am right on time for my children. My fellow Haitians I will reward you with everything if we change the way we live because I cannot fight alone. I need the strength of my people. I need the courage from the most, High. I do not need money, I need PEACE. I do not need money; I will give all of my money to build a prosperous nation because I cannot live with knowing that Haiti is in disaster. I cannot breathe if my children are dying from the dust that is meant for your religious practices. You have my children eating the dirt that you use for your religious purposes which cursed them forever with the intent of eating to die. You have made my children zombies that I have to wake up with salt. My children will not be victims anymore, my Haitians will no longer tolerate their bloodline to be transformed into skin and bone with flesh that stick to their ribcages. They treat dogs better than us! I am coming Haiti; I was already here but I had to plan out how to save our country. Remember my name, Kimberly Anicette.

Thank you. Merci.

Misa Hylton was very relevant with my dreams of my braille project and of being the most fashionable musician. Wardrobe is very significant in a musician's life because what you wear not only reflects your personality, but it is a form of art that collaborates with your image.

I wanted to work with the best of the best to gain insight on fashion that no one has seen before, but on a smaller spectrum for a clothing business line. This situation taught me not to chase people and not to depend on anyone to make my life positive as it will only be successful through me. I spent many years and still am finding peace within myself and the only way to accomplish that is by focusing on my talents and the bigger purpose of my existence.

Misa Hylton, a fraudster for Misa Hylton fashion academy and Misa Hylton 360 life coach proclaiming fashion studies to young women and life coach advice for $150 USD for a phone call that she does not come through for and pretends to reschedule which she does not come through for as well. Misa Hylton is a fraud because she took my money without my promised services, who knows how many countless people she has fabricated to help but goes on an overseas "trip". I did not give my hard-earned money as a hard working struggling young adult for life empowerment to be a victim of computer fraud. I visited the big apple, New York city on my own to locate Misa Hylton and ask her why she did not return my phone call that was rescheduled multiple times and to prove her I had talent as a future designer. I went on August 14th, 2018 only to find that Misa Hylton fashion academy did not exist! I was very hurt and shocked to realize I had been a victim of computer fraud.

I had the opportunity to work alongside Diddy for

his upcoming project making the band 2020 but was faced with challenges that made me realize that my lifelong dream of working for him was unnecessary for my come up. Individual come up is the new way artists sought for because of the royalties they earn through their music. I have a purpose with my music, and it does not matter who wants to be along side with me because in the end I will accomplish what I have set out to do. Being an independent artist gain 100% of their royalties which allows them full control of their art and how it connects to their individuality. Our mainstream music is polluted by guns, drugs, and sex which do not feed the mind of children who have the power to change the world. Since I was thirteen years old, I wanted to be signed by bad boy records, but those chances were slim because I did not have the financial aspects to make it happen. As I am older, I realize the best thing for me is to be in full control of my dreams because that will get me further to my destination. Being a well-known musician also heightens my chances of attending my dream school. I had a dream of becoming a nurse because my mother wanted me to pursue that career. It is simple to get a job as well as it is a very respectable occupation, but I failed my first term biology class by 3%. Most nurses do not tell you how stressful the courses are let alone a 16-hour shift and how most nurses are miserable with their jobs since they work so hard which develops neglectful nurses or nurses who kill. Apples Dreams is to go to Harvard law school;

Why Harvard? My favourite movie is legally blonde where everyone thinks you are unintelligent, but you are utterly unique and pleased to inform them of your greatness, but no one believes you because of the first presentation of your actions. Barack Obama as well as Michelle Obama attended and graduated from Harvard university. I am the female Martin Luther King (Mrs. MLK; my family's initials) by the time I am 35 years old I'm going to be giving motivational speeches through out the world in English and in Creole. Harvard would be pleased to have me attend their university because I will go down in history as the most notorious woman in the world therefore with education I will stay on the right path. The cure for cancer lies in the brain of someone who cannot afford education and I want to travel the world searching and building educational systems to find the cure and change many lives in the process. Many wealthy parents have paid their child's way to school without making any difference to the world around them. I want to cure cancer and HIV whilst defining the black lives matter movement by gathering intelligent people like myself who have the answers to my questions and equations. Harvard University would mean no one can judge my past and simply respect me and my truth. I have a dream that education will turn my Apple's dreams into a symbol around the world for food and education by Kimberly C. Anicette

Email to my nursing coordinator with no reply

Dear Nursing school coordinator,

You did not remember my name, though you instilled me not to forget yours.

Like the final straw on a camel, tempting me to consider closing up my nursing doors.

It's drifting through my mind that it's because of my complexion,

Having to work twice as hard, not going to lie it has me stressing.

Kimberly is my name, meaning of the royal forest

Many businesses to claim, my true success I put to rest... only for you to forget my name.

Apples dream is to be a wife and President of the United States. The person I decide to marry is the most significant aspect in my life and will have a high chance of being the first gentleman in history. My advice on marriage stems from my grade 9 business teacher who always spoke about his wife and asked us the million-dollar question on what the value of a wedding ring was. As some students yelled out the price tag and the size, I stayed quiet waiting for him to disclose the answer to which he said the value of a wedding ring is the VALUE of the union between two people, it has nothing to do with money. I will own 100 percent of my amazing inventions and businesses which will overflow my cup, filling the cup of my husbands, that will be the creation of two billionaires. I will not settle for being less than a wife, along with the solid mentality that I am *his* wife because I am worth every penny as I am an investment to my future love with every aspect. My prince charming and I will have a union of a business deal that vows to stay in business forever. I only want to be recognized as a one-man, woman to the world as he will be known as a one-woman, man. Faithfulness to my spouse relates to my faithfulness for my country, I believe. If I want to go down in history as one of the most powerful figures in the world I must have a particular partner who makes me feel secure on running a country.

Every girl dreams of the day they get married to their prince charming in their sparkling white dress. The man that will move mountains, conquer all evil and bring along snacks for the ride. As I sip on my Hi-C with my refined pallet, I unknowingly signaled that the way to my heart is through my stomach and I shall be all smiles (photo at the end of book).

Proverbs 18:22
²² He who finds a wife finds what is good and receives favor from the Lord.

The bible says a man must look for his wife with purpose and make preparation being equipped before the pursuit. I have been your wife in waiting before you have even given me the ring. I will help you with your vision, but you have the responsibility to lead me towards your aspirations in order for me to succeed in the assignment. You are the man who made me into the woman God called me to be, in order to fulfill your desires. You may already be equipped in life with material wealth, but true fundamental wealth is absent from your life. You must ask God to close your wounded flesh that he took your rib from to make me and be guided by your spirit. You must understand the substance I bring within my heart and not how I look in the flesh. I need to understand that you are a powerful man of God that has the substance to carry my oil to anoint your life. Ask God if I truly am the woman made from your rib because I was created to be found by you, I was born in the Jackson Memorial hospital for your purpose otherwise my heart would not have been strong enough to survive towards my first breath in Haiti. You must find me when you are ready because I was born to lead a nation.

5 promises to my husband and me

1. I promise to always listen to your thoughts and struggles with out disrupting you and believing the words that come out of your lips without judging you and without criticism by always being understanding.

2. I promise to remind you how much of an intelligent man you are, my King because I know you are more than capable of protecting me and our family THAT is why I love you the most; protection from my soldier.

3. I promise to let you be the man of the family because I believe you are capable of being an amazing provider to me and will thank you always for wearing the pants in the relationship as I do not care about material wealth, I care about saving the children.

4. I promise to always accept you and your past, present and future because I know who you truly are to this day and the growth you've accomplished. I know you are not what the media portrays you to be, you are a kind-hearted soul who deserves peace on Earth because you did not deserve to be abused by the ex girlfriend. You did not deserve that hurt.

5. I promise to always desire ONLY YOU because I know you are special and will accomplish all your dreams, leaving a legacy that is unmeasurable to any other man. I will give you all my tunnel vision and support everything you do.

Email to Misa Hylton 360 life coach

Misa Hylton 360 Transformation Coaching
Wed, Jun 6,
2018, 1:45PM
Greetings Kimberly,
Continued gratitude for your patience. We are doing

our best to schedule you as soon as possible, however, Ms. Hylton is currently preparing for a trip overseas, and we are currently scheduling calls for her return next week.

Please let us know if you will be able to schedule the week of June 12th, or June 19th.

We would like to remind you that Misa is Life Coach and not a psychologist. If you are experiencing feelings that you do not want to stay alive. We sincerely encourage you to connect with the suicide prevention resources in your area.

From: *coaching misahylton.com*
Date: *March 19, 2018 at 10:09:36 AM EDT*
To: *Kim Anicette*
Subject: Re: Life coach!!
Reply-To: *coaching misahylton.com*

Hello Kimberly,
Peace and Greetings!

Thank you for reaching out and taking the first step towards healing and creating the life that you desire. This is a powerful step that takes courage and commitment.

We are excited to announce new pricing for our coaching service with Ms. Hylton! If you would like to go forward, you would need to schedule a discovery session which costs $75. The discovery session starts with a questionnaire which must be filled out 48 hours before your session which lasts about 45 minutes to an hour. Once the discovery session is complete you may decide if you would like to move forward with life coaching services.

Please find our NEW pricing below, you can either go with the Coaching Package or a Single Session:

The Coaching Package consists of 3 sessions that span over a 3 month time period. This is the recommended path because it allows you to come full circle with your coaching experience in a timely matter. By the end of the 3 sessions, if your intent is set on getting the most out of your time with Misa, and following through with your plan, you will be well on your way to accomplishing your goals! The total for the Coaching Package is $300, with $150 being paid to startband $150 by the 5th of the 2nd month. (total 3 sessions, 1 session each month) If you would like more then 1 session a month that may be arranged. The Single Sessions offer more flexibility and for you to move forward on your own terms, which works best for some people. You can stop and go as you need to, and go beyond the 3 sessions if you need the extra support and coaching. The single sessions are $125 per session. Please let us know if you are interested in going forward and if so which option works best for you at this time and we will get you going with your next steps!

I look forward to hearing from you!

With Gratitude,

Coaching Coordinator 360 Transformation

On March 17, 2018 at 6:54 PM Kim Anicette wrote:
Hey Ms. Misa,

I've recently applied to your fashion academy but I'm a follower of yours on Instagram and I've been reading your inspirational pictures on this St. Patrick's Day. I would like to set an appointment with you because you are exactly what I need to move on from a troubled past of pain that I want to overcome. I want to live my best life and let go of my fears.

Thank you for listening
Have a good day,
Kimberly A

Emails from Misa Hylton

From: *Misa Hylton 360 Transformation Coaching*
Sent: *April 29, 2018 3:08 PM*
To:
Subject: *Your Next Steps with Misa!*

Separate emails to Bad Boy Records with no reply:

From: Kim Anicette
Sent: December 29, 2012 8:25 PM
To: harve.pierre@badboyworldwide.com <harve.pierre@badboyworldwide.com>; carla@badboyworldwide.com <carla@badboyworldwide.com>
Subject: Kimberly Anicette. please read.

Kimberly Anicette
Niagara Falls, ON Canada

Dear Bad Boy Records,

I am an African American 14 yr. old female would love to be signed by your label. After all of my research in the past, I believe that this label's work ethic is fantastic. I want to succeed in life, doing one of the things that make me happy. I am inspired by the people with this label, and other artists. I may be young, but my perseverance, and my genuine personality will always guide me with responsibility, and determination. I planned on trying to get signed by your label a year ago, but I was not confident in myself enough to think that I would have a chance. When I was younger, I always dreamed about doing something great in life to help my family. I was born in Miami, but also lived in Haiti for a short period of my life. Nothing in life that is worth something, comes easy. I believe and know that if I want to make my dreams into reality, I must work hard for what I want

I am always singing and trying to improve my singing skills. To be completely honest, I'm not like most teenagers. Most of my friends are always out going to parties, etc., but I'm always at home singing or listening to music. Such as Tupac, Luther Vandross, The Wolf, Jagged Edge, B.I.G, Cassie, Beyoncé, Rihanna, and more. I am interested in this label because the best of the best works with Bad Boys.

What is it about this label that I want to be signed? Well, The Wolf has worked for everything he has. In my eyes he is a legend, and one of my role models because he got to the top of the music industry because he believed in himself when times were hard. Even through all the fame, his first priority isn't being P. The Wolf. It's being The Wolf, father, family, and friend. Also, Notorious B.I.G., or known as Christopher Wallace has had a huge impact on Hip Hop. He came from nothing and made his talent worth something.

Therefore, I believe that this label has the right qualities to help me achieve my goals. No matter what I will always put God first.

Please reply, back if interested.

Sincerely,

Kimberly Anicette

***From:** Kim Anicette*
***Sent:** June 25, 2013 10:00 PM*
***To:** Kim Anicette*
***Subject:** Bad boys*

I am an African American 15 yr. old female would love to be signed by your label. Since I am in high school, I always sing in front of my classes. They're always saying who knew a voice like that would come out of me. They are always surprised and say that I should be a singer. I love performing in front of people, because they never expect me to be able to dance and sing too.

Therefore, I believe that this label has the right qualities to help me achieve my goals. No matter what I will always put God first. Please reply if interested. I want to take the chance because I don't want to look back in life thinking "what if"

2017

Although I am only 19 years old, my trials and tribulations have made me mature enough to focus on my long-term goals because I believe my purpose is to help and educate. My career goal is to be an author, teacher, mother, and President of the United States (If that is in Gods plans).

Therefore I want to educate children on different realities in the world with my foundation, while expanding my knowledge to write books as my asset, and becoming President of the United States by positively impacting the lives of not only children but children of color so they can change the world and leave behind a legacy that is unbreakable.

I just want to be the best version of myself and be HAPPY. I see myself being able to apply the skills I've learned at Misa Hylton Fashion Academy everyday with the unique knowledge gained for my foundation. I want to learn more about myself and my leadership skills while learning how to engage with diverse groups of people in the business aspect of my foundation.

Trafficking Tip Two: Mental Health

Mental health is your saving grace if you plan to exit. Your mentality will make or break you, it is as simple as that. If you let others talk you into making certain actions it will be harder to be in control. Your mind is what protects you from danger, if you put your trust in someone who makes you feel anything other than happiness it will be mentally exhausting and your body will follow. Clarity of the mind will ensure the best outcomes for your future.

Chapter 3 | Sunshine

A little girl who lost her grandfather at the age of 6 as she got home from school

WORDS CANNOT DESCRIBE how much I miss you, the day you took your last breath the sun was shining as I walked home from school. I was exposed to so much madness; lost and confused while I blatantly heard the horrible news of losing you. Only six years old therefore I did not understand but I felt as though my life was going to end. The hurt in my mothers' eyes revealed her deep pain and after that day it is safe to say I have never been the same. I blame poverty for taking my grandfather away from me because in the land of the free we have everything he needed. My own thoughts haunt me because I have no memories of him and when I slept death crept in my dreams. He was my sunshine, but he left me while the sun shined which caused my days to become dark because our bodies were permanently apart. He was "the Boss" now everything was lost, his leaving caused so much chaos that fear over grew in our minds and I paid the cost. If I could go back in time, I would bring him the medication he needed to survive. My life would be different, and things would not be the same but if that were the case then "Apple" might have never been my name. I owe my entire life to him and when I transition, I will be in search of him in the afterlife my sunshine, my light. I dream of the day we meet with arms wide open spiritually. He has given me so much purpose and I know without a doubt he watches over me and protects me from unknown darkness, but I must say living without him is the hardest. I have a dream and I am of his genes that brings beauty to all as a flower; beautiful and unique. He is my little soul in the sunshine, without him I am incomplete; finally, I understand why he named me Kimberly Cécille Anicette.

How do I feel when the sun hits my face? I love the warmth; I happen to only take long hot showers and they say people take long hot showers because they are lonely in life. I would agree. Maybe in my past life I electrocuted myself in the bath because I hate drinking water; but my mother says it is because I am a goat (Haitian goats do not drink much water). That's why

I have a business for supplying electricity to the world called Higher Power! But maybe you will only hear about it through this book; I am so sad I have been sad since my paternal grandfather died. You never forget how you find out a love one died, and my mother was so distraught that she told me he died with a voice full of anger since I could not understand her words the previous times. Shortly after my paternal grandfather transitioned our house was robbed, now the thought of being robbed terrifies me. That next few nights I could not sleep because the refrigerator was very loud, I thought it was a door opening as we slept on the living room floor. My mother told me I was supposed to be a twin but she transitioned after two heartbeats became one. To this day, I have a birthmark on my stomach of Pac man eating a small circle, that is my connection that she exists in the spiritual realm. Mother walked me to school where I looked up at the clouds only to see a child figure who I assume now was Beverly standing next to a man wearing a distinctively spiked rose thorn crown. As I walked closer there appeared to be more angels behind them in the hundreds. I drew it out at school, that is when I found out Jesus was real and I did have a sister, but mother did not believe me as I was just a kid until years later she told me about her experience learning she had lost my twin. When I was a younger girl I disliked going to school, I felt and envisioned there was supposed to be someone with me to go to school with me, switch seats and take hard tests for me. If I had my twin sister this world would not be able to sustain our minds, it is better that one of us is in the heavens for protection and guidance. I spend as much time as I can in the sun and often speak into it as if I were speaking to my transitioned loved ones. I'll write letters and meditate hard on what I want to manifest then burn them to let go of my wishes. My most important wish is who I will marry and continue my lifeline to sustain the legacy of my grandfathers.

Letter to my husband to be and me xo 8.9.18

Fri, Aug 10, 2018, 12:14 AM

Dear Kimberly and the one you choose to marry,

If you are reading this right now, then this must be the year of 2020 and everything I have wished for has come true. If I could predict your future, I would say the love of your life is Christopher Maurice Brown. I pray for you every day and pray you are successful in business and vibrate at an all-time high level. I pray you find and marry the man that takes away all your pain and loneliness. I hope he makes you SO happy and fills your heart with pure love, happiness, and peace. If you are reading this that means you are alive, and I am extremely happy you are alive. You just quit your job on my end in 8.9.2018 so I apologize for the mountains you must climb to be GREAT. The life I want for you is one that is generous, kind, and expensive. By this time, you should have struck a home run with your Check-it invention, you probably won the lottery for mother since her heart cannot handle such shock. I hope you are fit and dope with so much more potential left inside of you. Most importantly I pray that you continue putting your faith in God first and feel freedom on your skin. Life is hard and sometimes I do not want to carry on with it but make me proud for believing in myself and always putting myself first.

To my man,

I am thankful of who you are on the inside and I am thankful that the universe has placed you in front of me. I hope that I make you happy and you see your whole life in my eyes. I pray that you cherish me and love me with your heart on your sleeve because that is how I will be loving you. I pray we live our best lives and grow deeper and deeper in love with each other. I cannot wait for our child(ren) together and see your face when the moment comes. I pray you accept all my flaws and think being with me is a dream and if I could sing a song for you it would be I gotta be by Jagged Edge. Who ever you are I cannot wait to meet and be with you forever.
Love,
Kimberly Cécille Anicette

KC was planted in Haiti, sprouted her roots to Miami Florida, flourishing in Canada. Like a rose filled with thorns on the stems but a beautiful flower, I have flourished to be ME. I understand the meaning of TIME and DEDICATION similar to a plant that needs plentiful sunshine to sprout. I am fortunate to have grown up with necessities needed for survival that many in the world do not know is accessible. My family origin has made me humble and empathetic towards those who struggle to feed their families while living in a world filled with greed, hatred, and inequality. It is up to us as human beings to help those who lack everyday things that we take for granted for example hot showers with privacy and the ability to have a good toothbrush at hand. My mother worked extremely hard so I would never go hungry like she did as well as give me better opportunities she did not experience such as an education, especially in the category of free tuition. My mother gave up her comfortable life for me so that I could get the education she never received. As her first born she risked it all just so I could have the opportunities Haitians are robbed of; such as education simply because they could not afford it. Teachers in Haiti are strict and demand respect from their students; being late will bring upon punishment resulting to being smacked on the hands with a ruler or other similar forms of discipline. Nail polish is not allowed and will result in the painful ruler discipline or get you suspended until it is taken off. Every student must recite the previous lesson from the day before otherwise they will be disciplined. Uniforms are mandatory with respected colours; my maternal grandmother chose to be a single parent therefore she could not afford uniforms for my mother along with her three siblings and would sew the uniforms herself. My mother would walk two hours to get to class and two hours back home for her school break, when I was complaining about a ten-minute fast walk to my high school. The circumstances I have encountered have shaped me to be the person I am, well beyond my years and I am thankful for everything my mother has done for me. Save Haiti KC is dedicated to my mother and Haitians for all their hardships, tribulations but also their compassion and hope for a better environment. My only dream in life is to give back for everything that was endured and rebuild Haiti, the beautiful land of mountains.

IT IS TIME TO EAT.

How did my parents meet? They were in the same church choir but never noticed each other until one big gathering with food, and entertainment but it was cancelled due to heavy rain which causes deadly flooding on the streets. My father asked my mother to cook for him since he saw what she brought and my mother accepted, she was in shape (you could stack a cup on the arch of her back), such great shape my father noticed her immediately out of her choir uniform. Their second date was to a small local restaurant where the couple next to them were saying they were craving to eat BBQ in a high-class way. My parents were so poor, they did not know what barbeque was and asked each other if they knew what it meant; that is when they fell in love, making it their mission to try barbecue together one day; they were so poor they did not know barbeque was simply smoked meat! Now barbeque is a luxury to me because of this prized story of my parents and those in Haiti who can not afford to add fire to their food.

Matthew 5:6

6 Blessed are those who hunger and thirst for righteousness, for they will be filled.

The bible says those who are hungry for righteousness will be filled, meaning it is about spiritually finding happiness in things that do not require materialistic wealth but to change the world and fight for others who starve by acting in righteousness pursuing the Lord to accomplish the will he has placed in our hearts.

Haiti is the poorest country in the western hemisphere. Haiti is filled with beautiful mountains, but unfortunately, there are poverty-stricken areas with the threat of waste to the environment. Dirt cookies are made from hand mixing dirt, water, salt, and sunlight. Since majority of the population lives without electricity, the sun is used to dry the cookies for consumption. Clean water is not always accessible therefore salt is used for flavour. Children are forced to survive in areas where there is no proper garbage disposal. Imagine the ground you walk on is also what you consume? Slaves were fed one hand full of soup or pieces of bread. Now some only have dirt and time which molds the cookie shapes dry. Even though it does little for them they still are thankful for having something to eat. Women have the roles of cooking but there are times when they wake up and go to bed hungry. Some children would get 1 small plate of rice, sauce, fish, and a small cup of water for the whole day. Then come back begging because they are hungry; eat for the day or save and pray?

Story telling in Haiti is a huge entertainment. Some people must watch television through the window of their neighbors. Imagine watching the super bowl as a peeping Tom! When night falls the whole family would gather around and tell scary stories or stories to teach the kids life lessons. Stories were told mostly to educate the kids in a fun positive way and to teach right from wrong. Education is a privilege that many parents cannot afford, and strict teachers will test you to your fullest abilities. Those who are fortunate to go to school yet are careless with their studies will be kicked out immediately. Students must recite their previous lessons word for word to the teacher, or they will have to re-write it out until it is embedded in their brain. It took me a long time to realize the sacrifices my mother made for me so that I could be here today. I was always ashamed of the fact that my mother was a foreigner who had a thick accent when speaking English, but she was trying. I never invited friends over because I was ashamed that I did not live in a huge house when there are people who live in plastic tents in Haiti and all over the world. I later learned that my parents housed struggling students in Haiti who otherwise would be living on the streets. I was upset that I could not get help with my homework because the curriculum is different. I never once thought about all she had to give up, so I could live a better life. I always had food to eat and a place to sleep, even if that meant she would go hungry herself or work even harder. My mother earned the chance to go on a business trip to Miami, Florida for a week, and had me 1 month premature but more on that in Chapter 4. God works in mysterious ways because if I were born in Haiti, my chances of being alive today would be zero due to the earthquake. Haiti will always be my second home because of the battles my family faced to get where we are today. My family is respected and well known in the communities we live in.

We all have our own stories that make us unique; whether coming from a rich or poor background, we all have the potential to do good in this world. Nelson Mandela once said, "education is the most powerful weapon which you can use to change the world." My family was once the poorest of poor and now we own multiple houses and schools in gated communities throughout Port au Prince, and Tigauve, Haiti. Most of the people in Haiti do not own cars which results in walking or taking crammed busses. A common folklore told is not to judge a book by its cover; a person can be in an expensive car while you are walking past you notice it and are upset you have to walk, when in reality they have a broken AC and are dying of heat while you are surrounded by fresh air.

Depending on their location, students would prepare for a 2-3 hour walk to school on dangerous pathways. When I was younger, my parents would arrange someone to walk me to school as they went to work. I was spoiled; of course, therefore I would always demand to be carried instead and would not share my Cheetos or other snacks and would perform a common Haitian dance called La Loze if I was asked to share. Breakfast is known to be the most important meal of the day, yet Haitian students go about their whole day on an empty stomach. Some schools provide one bowl of rice and beans, children are often malnourished with no access to clean water, which results in a high rate of sickness and death.

1 John 3:17-18
17 If anyone has material possessions and sees a brother or sister in need but has no pity on them, how can the love of God be in that person? 18 Dear children, let us not love with words or speech but with actions and in truth.

The bible says those who have many to offer to the world but choose to be selfish will not be rewarded by God. For myself, I may speak on the changes I want to produce onto the world, but it will be my actions that dictate that God is working through me for a better change. My dreams, my truth, will change the lives of many who need help and hope which will bring love to the world that we live in and slowly bring on the changed world our children deserve to live in. I see this book as an investment to those who can afford it but those who cannot, will be rewarded through my actions gaining faith in my mind, body, soul, and purpose.

PARTNER$HIP

Fri, Mar 16, 2018, 4:49 PM

Hello!

I am a huge fan of Chris Brown and I would love to partner with this clothing label Black Pyramid because it brings out the exact message and vision, I have for my dream of connecting the Haitians and Black Community. I have been working on this project for 3 years now and this is the cherry on top of my foundation. I have BIG goals for myself and I am very selective with the clothes I wear. Sponsoring and distributing your brand will increase sales and connect BLACK Teens/Pre adults as well as those who stand with the BLACK LIVES MATTER movement. I am a ridiculously hard worker and I am confident that this is my decade for POSITIVE success. Haitian Flag Day is May 18th, my birthday is May 23 and I need something dope to incorporate with my Foundation; Black Pyramid is a future investment of mine.

The Kissing Booth was created regarding myself

(Kimberly Cécille Anicette) who gives 3 kisses to the sky whenever I leave my house. One day I will get married to the love of my life, and soulmate which will be sealed with one kiss for eternity. The Kissing Booth will be a business venture for those who are ready to propose to their significant other as well as oral hygiene and hot meals for the less fortunate who lack necessities that result to them not taking care of their smiles. The Kissing Booth was inspired by my biology teacher who taught me the importance of the digestive system. As a scientist she explained what occurs in your body when you have a meal to eat with such precision in her education. My biology teacher Mrs. Booth inspired me to create a triple meaning company that will be dedicated to the homeless and men wanting to propose to their future wives, and beauty products for women, separately. Mrs. Booth was there for me during the darkest times of my high school career by holding my hand through depression and suicidal thoughts that came about because the school told me I would not graduate. Mrs. Booth is the saint that saved my life when the very people I worked for as a student giving informative speeches about Haiti increasing their Apple pie sales, donations and singing to the entire school body, explained I had no community service hours when I had in fact completed 40+ hours prior to reaching grade 12. The Kissing Booth is dedicated to Mrs. Booth for being an angel in disguise helping me get the mental help I needed to battle my depression and walk the stage at graduation. I did not take my high school graduation photos because of this incident as well as the fact that I was not given my honour roll documentation and credibility as I walked across the stage and was told to pick up the certificate the following day. Regardless of the treatment I faced as a student at my high school, this is where I was told by the strictest principle of the origins of my last name, Anicette being an Italian Liqueur but realized it was spelled differently. Thank you to the principle who gave me this piece of knowledge to start my own liqueur business and have my name competing with the best alcoholic beverages in the world, as well as being able to be paired with coffee, the symbolic beverage in Haiti that many cannot afford.

LETTER TO GOD, 2018

I am making a new list of what I want in my life and in a man. Although my ideal man would be Christopher Maurice Brown, I am willing to wait for your blessing for my future husband and father of my children. Firstly, of course, I must praise you and give you thanks for not giving up on me when I was giving up on myself these years.

I am trusting you and the universe that my life will be worth all the troubles I have been through. I want to help people the way you helped those who needed you. What I want for myself is to be genuinely happy every day and not dread through life like its just another day.

I want to bring peace to others and make someone else's day worth living.

I want flowers planted in the darkest parts of my mind reassuring that I was once blind but now can see. I want you to guide me in fulfilling my dreams of bringing peace to those who have nothing but the dirt you used to make Adam. I want to be free of all debt, meaning lingering friendships, relationships, and money. I want to be radiating my happiness from inside, out. I want to be healthy in every aspect of my body and life. I want to have a true genuine bright smile that represents the level and energy I am on. I want to be cleared of my depressions and anxiety and fear of the world around me. I want to be viewed as a hero to many people who need my help. I want to be treated like royalty regarding my worth and my ability to love and provide for my culture. I want to be ridden of all evil that remains in my mind and body, I want to forgive myself for my past and present. I want to be remarkably successful and a worldwide icon for peace. I want abundance for love, peace, and beautiful hair. I want my skin to glow when I see the face of who is meant for me. I want to feel your energy and simply know it is him when I see him. I want to be rich, so rich to save the country of Haiti and destroy poverty. 2 BILLION dollars would provide access to my dreams and the simplicity of changing decades of lives.

My future husband:

FIRSTLY, HE NEEDS TO BE A MAN OF GOD.

I want him to want to settle down and want to be a husband and father more children. I want him to constantly remind me how much he loves me, and I want him to confide in you when temptation occurs and when he needs someone to hear him out when I am not there. I want him to be a leader and protect our family no matter the circumstances. I want him to want to be with me rather other women who come his way. I want him to have learned from his past mistakes and recognize he is not perfect but puts in the effort to prove his love and loyalty. I never want him to feel like physical, mental, and emotional abuse is the answer to whatever test we encounter. I want our love to be so pure and true that we pray to overcome obstacles. I want him to be all that he is and accept all that I am. I want him to have fun with me and laughter be the medicine to whenever we fight or disagree on something. I want him to spoil me with positivity and gifts that he knows will make me happy. Even the smallest gestures from him will make me happy showing that he cares. I want him to be very honest with me knowing what is done in the dark will come to light. I want him to feel as if time stops when he is with me and is obsessed with being in love with me because I make him so happy. I want him to own up to his mistakes when they are made and not be afraid to show and tell me when he is wrong. I want him to always have my best interests and stick up for me when I am disrespected behind my back. I want him to go to war for me and our family. I want him to trust me more than he loves me and values our friendship and relationship to the ultimate degree. I want him to claim me when the sun is out and when the moon shines. I want him to be confident that the woman I am is more than enough and will not dare to ruin anything we have between us. I want him to be private with our business. I want him to be forgiving of his past pains and love his mother making sure she respects me and loves me as if I were her daughter and spoils me with love. If he has children, I pray they accept me into their heart and love me as if I were their mother and spoil me with love. I want him to be obsessed with loving me and making love to me whenever he can. I want him to WANT me to bear his children as MANY AS POSSIBLE. I want him to be faithful when I am pregnant with his children and love me even more because I am bringing life into this world that is a mixture of us. I want him to communicate with me on everything and run everything by me for my opinion and support. I want him to be clean internally and externally. I want to be the center of his world. I want him to be romantic and passionate falling in love with me every time he sees me. I want him to be so in love with me that I am covered in him and he is covered in me endlessly. I want us to reflect each other with nothing but love and happiness. I want no enemies to succeed in any mission they plan to destroy us. I want him to be patient in our love and with me as I will with him. I want him to WANT to marry me and make me his forever. I want us to be rich in every aspect of our lives being money (billions), financially, spiritually, mentally, emotionally, and family/ friend wise.

Love,

Kimberly Cécille Anicette

Sunny Booth is an invented charity by Kimberly that will feed the homeless through out the USA and Haiti onto the world during the times that breakfast is consumed as well as plant trees for oxygen and food while touring to different cities for music, business, or vacation. C.E.O. stands for Currently Elevating Oxygen. Breakfast is the most important meal of the day and the darkest hour is just before dawn; meaning you may have gone through dark times but even the sun must rise after a thunderstorm. We greet the sun by stretching our limbs and yawning. We continue greeting the sun because time does not exist, each day forward is one step closer to the life you have never imagined, perseverance is critical because life will test your strength and reward you if you pass the test.

G.U.N. to G.U.M. was created regarding gun violence in America which is very prominent due to the blue collared employees. Blue collared crimes have been acceptable for centuries; now is the time to change the system. G.U.N. stands for Girls Uniting Niggas

G.U.M. refers to the Black Lives Matter movement or the Blackout movement in the music industry meaning Girls Uniting by Mouth. As a musician signed to OHB I will use my voice to speak on the injustices that black people and Police officers face daily. I want to save both black lives as well as differentiate the GOOD blue collared police officers from the evil blue collared police officers. When I am President, I will re-evaluate gun laws in America to decrease the number of homicide rates caused by bullet wounds. Those who willingly turn in their guns will be rewarded with a cash value to start businesses, pay off their mortgage, especially those who live in the hood to open up black owned real estate. Only police officers will be able to carry a concealed weapon which will allow more black people to consider entering the police force. It will be illegal for police officers to kill unarmed black men and women and organize how civilians use firearms. This will spark my (L)OVE business meaning lungs to ovaries for mothers and wives who do not get the chance to procreate the next generation because their loved ones were fatally shot. (L)OVE is my invention and solution to take control of the Black Lives Matter movement and gang wars, hence why I call myself the Black Medusa with the slogan HANDS UP, SO THEY DON'T SHOOT YA a term I will be known for as a lawyer when I look into the eyes of anyone who is guilty of killing an unarmed person.

Trafficking Tip Three: Protection

Protection from your pimp is only valid when they are in the same vicinity as you to react. Many pimps will only protect you if you are giving them money, otherwise you are alone and will need to protect yourself. The starting price for protection is $10, 000. This is a tactic to secure your worth to your pimp that your life is of value if conflict arises.

Chapter 4 | 523

*Happy Birthday! What is
your purpose little girl?*

OUR FATE IS set in stone from the moment of conception to the moment of our last breath yet what matters most is the time in between called life. Free will allows us to choose our battles but not the consequences of our actions. The universal symbol of balance is the Yin and Yang, perfectly representing the good within the bad and the bad within the good. Life is a simulation of puzzle pieces that ultimately makes sense when life flashes before our eyes painting our perfect picture. Patience is the skill to master as we all wait for the outcomes of our plans, inevitably what will be, will be.

My mother's first pregnancy was terminated during

the early stages of her second trimester due to a strong blow to her ankle which resulted to the lost soul of my brother. Miscarriages are common during pregnancy and generally occurs for reasons outside the mothers' control and nothing can be done to prevent or stop it from happening. The following year in September of 1997 I was conceived as a birthday gift, passing me on to be her rainbow baby and first child. While at my mothers' ultrasound screening during her first trimester the doctor informed her that she would be having identical twins as two heartbeats were seen. During the second trimester my mother would be a victim of vanishing twin syndrome as there was only one heartbeat implying that my fetus absorbed the fetal tissue of my twin in the womb while discovering I would be her daughter. Summer of 1998 my mother earned the final representative seat for her archives company's overseas conference meeting in Miami, Florida along with a few of her colleagues for a seven-day business trip with all expenses paid. Employees (mostly men) demanded to take her place since she was 8 months pregnant with my fetus in her womb, which her boss disregarded since my mother was an expert typist and he had firmly made his decision and she was barely showing since she carried small. Due to my "on my terms" character, on the final night in the hotel hours before the scheduled flight back to Port-au- Prince, Haiti as she was packing her suitcase, her water broke and those in the room panicked alerting the other colleagues causing more chaos dramatically exclaiming "Oh Lord, why is it NOW this woman must have her child?". My mother was in complete shock as she had no one to drive her to the hospital let alone no support system in the USA slowly and unknowingly causing her blood pressure to rise. My birth date was due in late June and had I waited a couple hours that night, I would have been born on the plane in dangerous circumstances but at the least I would have gained free airfare for life or gained my wings joining my beloved sister. My mother arrived at the Jackson Memorial Hospital in Miami Florida and nurses rushed her into the delivery room, connecting her to monitors as fast as possible. Speaking very little English my mother understood how serious my delivery would be as the chatter increased yet the room was silent, with nurses and doctors rushing in and out, time stood still as she heard no heartbeat. "lub-DUB, lub-DUB, lub-DUB" she faintly heard my symphony only to disappear in and out. The obstetrician told her I was a premature baby with a premature heart beat therefore if she wanted to save my life they would have to perform an emergency Caesarean section as her life was in danger as well with the threat of preeclampsia which would impair the organs in my body. She agreed yes and within minutes they rushed her to the emergency operating room where they made an incision in my mother's abdomen and uterus, with her bladder and intestines moved aside allowing the surgeon to better see and reach my fetus. My mother felt sensations described as pulling and pressure as she was barely awake and numbed from the waist down due to the dosage of anesthesia. Hearing no cries, they rushed me to the NICU to restart my heart thus bringing me back to life then placing me in an incubator separating me from my mother for three days. The operation of a Caesarean section delivery lasts from fifteen to twenty minutes and forty minutes to stitch the deep wounds. My mother became very weak, cold, and could not walk, let alone travel to the top floor to spend time with her newborn baby. Once my mother gained the strength to walk to the elevator, she was terrified since it was her first time ever encountering such a machine and she felt the vibrations ripping through her fresh wound. The nurse asked my mother what would she name me and my mother replied "Mary Cécille" to which the nurse politely said to keep Cécille but that Mary was an elderly woman's name making my mother laugh and put off giving me a name for months telling the hospital she would reach them with a name via paperwork. Mary was my aunt who passed away in Haiti due to voodoo a co-worker had placed on her, I wish I could have met her, but she is better off in heaven with my warriors of angels protecting me.

As a child I did not understand that after death life continues, but I did know that "people" could stand on clouds and even fly next to them. 6 lapses around the sun until darkness grew deep in my mind. I would go back in time to that day and tell myself my grandfather is still with me, I just could not see him, people love you easily when it is too late. I had no recollection of my grandfather before this traumatic experience, but he knew me. Both of my grandfathers had nicknames, being the King (maternal) and the Boss (paternal). The day of the Boss' passing the sky was blood orange and yellow making a beautiful sunset, I remember staring out the window every day afterschool wondering why time was so slow? While waiting for the sun to set. I have heard stories about him and how much he loved the stars in the sky in Haiti and how he hated carnivals, parties, and street games because it caused him to be late for work one day so he vowed to never participate in those activities. My favourite story told about the Boss is that he predicted there would be a President in the family bloodline, therefore no one can stop me from accomplishing my dream and the only connection I have to the Boss. This is what I call the Roaring 20's 2.0 you will know the name Kimberly C. Anicette 15 years from now. "The King" died a couple days after I sent him a text message thanking him for my beautiful hair that I had due to his genetics, to which I did not know that his response would be the last time I would be able to talk to him and for that I am grateful. Each morning for school we would recite the national anthem and something deep inside me admired how the American flag looked blowing through the wind; so much I would stop to admire the stripes and stars, I knew it had to be a major significance to me I just had to wait for time to reveal my destiny. I somehow remember being on my grandfathers the boss' farm with his chickens which was validated on my trip to Haiti for my sweet sixteenth birthday present to see how they live in poverty. My grandfather was right, the night skies in Haiti are the most beautiful skies I have ever witnessed, It made me feel connected to him especially visiting his and my grandmothers tombs that he built with his hands. I was told even after you die you still have a birthday. I was shocked that our loved ones can still be connected to us with such importance. Opinions of what heaven is like is different between everyone, but I believe it exists as well as I would like to believe that heaven has no pain.

I was named Kimberly by my grandfather and it is an English baby name meaning from the wood of the Royal Forest. From the royal fortress meadow. Cécille is derived from the Roman Cecilia name which is based on the Latin meaning blind. I will lead the blind because my eyes are open as well as provide access to braille and products for those who are vision impaired. The name was a third century Christianity who founded a church in the section of Rome. The story of her life was written, and she was regarded as a patroness saint of musician who sang to the heavens when she got married. Anicette, also called anise is a small star shaped fruit with one seed in each arm. The said flavour is of black liquorice as well as a spice in Asian cooking with it's flavour having similarities with other spices, such as star anise, and fennel. In Creole I am called "belly" or berly which is pronounced bellé Meaning beauty. In numerology the number 23 experts as a personal sense of freedom. Angel number 23 is made up of energies and attributes of the number two and three. Two added by three equals five. As humans we have five senses which are touch, taste, smell, sight, and hearing.

Urban dictionary's top definition of Kimberly means beautiful sweet and caring girl she is the most unique girl in the world, and she is definitely eye candy. There is no one like her but there is only one that she will always love there is one guy that will always change the way she feels because she is determined to only stay with one guy. Kimberly's are loyal, trusting, and down to earth. Kimberly's enjoy the simple things in life, if you catch one, you are a lucky person. Anyone dating Kimberly hit jackpot in the lottery. Her smile brightens up the whole room and her laugh adds more beauty to her. Born in the Jackson Memorial Hospital, Kim flipped backwards with an E at the end is Mike. One day through my music I would love to depict the Haitian culture of being the first black led republic and their history of zombies similar to Michael Jackson's Thriller. My mothers favourite colour has always been brown, the colour of her skin and eyes. Such beautiful brown with red tinted eyes she has! At birth she jokingly denied me as her daughter because of my distinctive almond shaped eyes, to this day she comments on my eyes as a baby calling them "ripped". I believe eyes are the best assets on a human, even those who are blind or with cataracts. Medusa was a beautiful mythology creature who turned into a monster after being a rape victim being a sexualized symbol of women's rage that would turn men to stone if they gazed into her eyes. I am able to tell if a man or woman is lying simply by looking into their eyes because as they say the eyes are the windows to the soul. I like to believe we all have a special purpose in our lives which is already planned out for us it all depends on us to make a mark in this world hoping and helping as many people as we can or let the gift of life slip through your fingers.

Black pyramid is a clothing brand founded by The Legend the meaning behind the name is the complex knowledge behind the pyramids and how they came to be. Egyptian pyramids were built for the country's pharaohs during the time of the third dynasty when Egypt was one of the richest and most powerful civilizations in the world. Although it is unknown how the pyramids were built, the remains of Kings were found in tombs as a key to learning more about ancient Egypt, the greatest mystery on earth. We do know Pyramids acted as giant power plants generating consistent energy for light. Haitian pyramids were formed as a result of the earths tectonic plate smashing together due to nonstop geologic movement below the surface. Haiti was one of the richest nations in the world during the time of slavery because of exploitation of indigo, sugar, coffee, and cotton. Black pyramid is black power understanding how important our culture shapes our future as the cycle of generations continue to evolve therefore, we need to feed ourselves from the inside out. Many know the story of Pocahontas a native descent of the Powhatan Tribe associated with the colonial settlement of Jamestown, Virginia in May 14, 1607 where the crop of tobacco was in demand leading the first documented Africans to be slaved in 1619 by capture of Portuguese ships. Haiti has a similar noble woman of the town of people who were indigenous of the Caribbean in Florida living in simplicity on the island of Haiti by fishing and farming. I will be the new hero for Haiti with my selfless acts of kindness which is my God's given purpose because the only person who can save Haiti is a Haitian herself not the Red Cross, more on that in the blanket theory by Kimberly Anicette.

In human nature, we neurologically awaken to the light of the sun and sleep to the glowing of the moon despite our location. Yawning and a rumbling stomach is our brains mechanism signaling that we need to eat nutritious food to maintain proper bodily function. Breakfast is believed to be the most important meal of the day to ensure high energy by eating foods with protein and fiber to maintain your appetite for the rest of the day. Those who tend to go without breakfast are susceptible to increased risk for heart disease, obesity, high blood pressure, high cholesterol, and diabetes

My P.L.A.N. (People Leading A Nation) is to:

- Collect and distribute Non- perishable food items that only need water added for consumption

- Rebuild homes in Port- au Prince for those who went homeless

- Introduce Financial Education to Haitians

- Produce profitable Solar Energy

I believe that if we stand together then we can rebuild Haiti into the beautiful land of mountains it once was. Children are our future, therefore, its time to start educating them on different realities so we can change the world. We need to teach children proper values and how to love not only themselves but each other and to not see race as an issue because we all look the same on the inside and when we transition. If we can teach children peace, then we can build a country with a solid foundation. Creole is a language that originates from pain… this is why it is my plan to kill the pain of hunger worldwide.

Introduction for my purpose as the President of the United States of America, 2017

I am CEO and President Kimberly Cécille Anicette, daughter of Haitian parents reiding in Niagara Falls, Ontario. I began my career in entrepreneurship at the age of 10 after the catastrophic magnitude 7 earthquake in Haiti on January 12, 2010. Later organizing a non- profitable foundation, my elementary school made efforts to aid those in need which earned me front page in the Niagara Falls Review local newspaper. I began writing informative speeches due to my passion for Haiti inspiring fellow teachers and classmates on my culture. Fast forward 3 years, I partnered with my Catholic Highschool and began educating my peers on the lifestyles of Haitians noticing a significant boost in our school's pilgrimage charity for Haiti. My speeches became known as legendary and uplifting for those who heard, those who missed it were informed about my talents. My dream is to take the knowledge I've gained over time amplifying my influence for a country then the entire world.

"What if the cure for cancer is in the mind of someone who can't afford an education?"

I believe that the FUTURE is FEMALE, and that female is HAITIAN. I plan on running for President of the United States of America as I will be eligible during the year of 2035 at the age of 37. Due to my experiences I have been through during my lifetime and my characteristics, I am able to rapidly contribute to multiple perspectives and realities than most teenagers. As a Haitian I am hungry for change and freedom, therefore the only choice I have is to become the ultimate boss by becoming President and uplifting my country with no distractions. I come from the jungle that paved the way to freedom for millions. It is in my DNA to pave the way to freedom for millions to come.

Although it is unknown how the Egyptians built the

pyramids, the remains of tombs found with Kings buried is the key to learning more about ancient Egypt. In Christianity, Jesus was placed in a tomb after his death, A tomb is a house to protect the dead and provide the deceased with a dwelling equipped with necessities for the afterlife.

Black power is understanding how important our culture shapes our future. As the cycle of generations continue to grow our children should be equipped with necessities for their lifetime. Laying a brick each day has the same effect as a butterflies wings creating a storm on the other side of the world. Our minds are our temples; therefore, we need to feed ourselves from the inside out and feed each other.

THE BLANKET THEORY by Kimberly Anicette

The blanket theory explained:

When I was around the age of 11 a group of mentors came to my school and took the class to the gymnasium and laid out two blankets on the floor. Separating us into two groups, we were told to stand on each blanket and as a team and flip it over with only one exception: No one could touch the ground or fall off the blanket. As everyone froze in confusion, I told everyone on my blanket to quickly squeeze together leaving half the blanket empty. I told half the students to step onto the other side slowly until the last person would allow me to twist the other side over. Success. The meaning of this is UNITY: Joined to accomplish the goal.

Apple's dream is to convert Haiti from rags to riches. There is no way to remove the entire population and reconstruct the country, therefore, it should be done in increments until the whole population is covered. For example, mail delivery UPS (United Parcel Service) or even your local newspaper delivery system covers a wide range of private subscribed neighborhoods in detailed coordination. Adding simple factors such as garbage, food, shelter, water, and clothing will build a functioning and lucrative nation it once was and more.

Life revolves around our hands and quite literally can be seen in our palms. Like a woman who keeps her temple beautifully kept my gift is to create a nail polish that detects each one of the three main date rape drugs.

GHB

- Comes as a liquid with no odor or color, white powder, and a pill.

- Takes effect in about 15 minutes and can last 3 or 4 hours

Symptoms Include:

- Loss of consciousness

- Drowsiness

- Dizziness

- Nausea
- Problems seeing

Ketamine

- Comes as a liquid and a white powder.
- Very fast-acting

Symptoms Include:

- Distorted perceptions of sight and sound
- Lost sense of time and identity
- Out of body experiences
- Dream-like feeling
- Feeling out of control
- Impaired motor function
- Problems breathing

Rohypnol

- Comes as a pill that dissolves in liquids.
- Effects can be felt within 30 minutes of being drugged and can last for several hours

Symptoms Include:

- Drunk feeling

- Problems talking

- Nausea

- No memory of what happened while drugged

- Loss of consciousness

- Confusion

Intuition is the ability to understand something immediately, without the need for conscious reasoning. It may come in the form of a dream, Deja vu, a funny feeling, or something else. Never doubt this feeling. Ever. My intuition came in a deep dark feeling in my heart that my death was approaching, and I unknowingly informed my rapist of all my fears of wanting to leave but he told me to stay. The moment God speaks to you if there are many distractions in your life you will not hear him. As a Haitian, I am very spiritual about every aspect of my life because I know everything belongs to a Higher Power. Ketamine, GHB, and Rohypnol are very potent drugs that are used for no other reason but for evil and when alcohol is in added, your body sinks into a dark hole.

*Overdose of these drugs may slow down breathing and heart activity eventually causing death

God must have a sense of humor because the most

challenging season of my life happens to be my breakthrough. "Write the vision, and make it plain upon tables, that he may run that readeth it. 3 For the vision is yet for an appointed time, but at the end, it shall speak, and not lie: though it tarry, wait for it; because it will surely come, it will not tarry." Habakkuk 2:2-3) Kimberly meaning Royal forest is the perfect example being "God never made not one chair nor a table. Hepi made a tree, and the rest is up to us. When God sends you a tree you imagine a table, a chair, a wall in the room, or a log cabin. Teenage and adult women to determine if their alcohol has been poisoned with date rape drugs. I will change the world with innovation and delivery of nail polish and items that detect those drugs.

Chemical and thermal reactions will be particularly important with my nail polish to decipher dangerous beverages as well as taking caution to extremely hot beverages. In colors of the rainbow Red, Orange, Yellow, Green, Blue, Purple, and Pink will be available in their darkest to lightest shades which will save millions, soon billions of lives globally.

The 14th Amendment to the US Constitution (July 9, 1868) states, "All persons born or naturalized in the United States, and subject to the jurisdiction thereof, are citizens of the United States and of the State wherein they reside." The concept is straightforward: those born in America are citizens, even if their parents are not. #45 wants to end birthright citizenship, which would deny citizenship to the American-born children of unauthorized immigrants and possibly to foreigners in the country on non-permanent visas. The urgency of "Make America Great Again" disentangles from simple xenophobia: the fear of immigrants changing the character of America and overrunning it's (white) population as an issue relies on fears about irreversible cultural change. Number 45 has made disparaging comments about Haiti and is building a wall between USA and Mexico. Children of Mexican and/or African American descent will be the future of our country who will rewrite history for the greater good. With all the innocence in the world, we must not damage the minds of our future leaders because who knows what force they will bring when they demand peace.

"6 Start children off on the way they should go, and even when they are old, they will not turn from it." (Proverbs 22:6)

I want my life to be a solution for women, the African American community especially Haitians, those struggling with poverty, and human rights. If I can plant a seed in the mind and hearts of Haitians as well as in the soil they walk on, my purpose will come to light and expand throughout the nations. I want to tailor my life precisely to the things that are necessary to where I am trying to go. I am willing to leave behind everything that does not serve me or God by breaking into a higher law to fulfill my dream of becoming President of the United States.

Thank you,

Kimberly Cécille Anicette

Apple's 3.14 Bakery 143 will be dedicated to her as a result to her significance in my life

An apple a day keeps the doctor away. An edible a day keeps the stress away! By Kimberly Anicette

Apple's bakery is Haitian female owned operating in Ontario Canada, the second and largest country in the world to legalize cannabis nationwide. Specializing in pies, soft brownies, chewy cookies, cupcakes, etc in both edibles' THC infused or non-edibles free of THC of your choice, all products are handmade and peanut-free. Cakes are available in multiple flavours and special orders are accepted upon request. Smoking cannabis is a combustion with 50 to 60% of THC it requires 10 minutes and rapidly dissipates over the next 30 to 60 minutes. Edibles require no combustion but instead requires patience and heat giving a more intense high with 10 to 20% of THC which is a healthier alternative. Being Haitian owned we have firsthand knowledge on the environment and lifestyles of Haitians in poverty. We stand for a greater purpose which is eliminating poverty in the country that was the most prosperous in the world. As a result, consuming or inhaling cannabis the main side effect is developing "munchies" a term used to explain is suddenly increased appetite. Honouring the new legalization Canadian apples will be used to create a special dish and apple pies in both edibles' THC infused or non-THC infused apple pies. There are endless possibilities of products made from an apple those products will feed Haitians replacing dirt cookies! How can the mind find peace when there is no peace in the tummy? Haiti is a land in the mountains located in the Western hemisphere sharing the island of Hispaniola known as the Dominican Republic in the Caribbean. Haiti is the first Black led republic in the world, yet children suffer due to high poverty rates. Since 80% of the population live without food and or electricity. When the power of love overcomes the love of power there will be peace. The purpose of baked cookies is to bring awareness to those in Haiti who consume cookies made from dirt, water, and sunlight. Those three essential ingredients are composed of the human nature and Adam and Eve's flesh. Who have been told they would die if they ate from the tree a pattern now followed by all the humans. God made one of every human from one mitochondrial X therefore, unity within humanity will give our children and generations to come to the foundation of the indigo world. The flag of Haiti is a bi color blue and red due to Haitians dark past from their rebellion against slavery for the purpose of black history. When yellow is included it produces the primary colours of light creating white and black knowing history repeats itself our unity can bring light to the minds of children who hold the key to saving our country. Clothing products Higher Power will be available for purchase in support of Apples & Sunshine an organization purposed to find and fund clothing, food, and shelter businesses in connection to Haiti.

Higher Power will ensure that children all over the world get access to education, electricity and food thus eliminating hunger worldwide. Food motivates those who do not have anything to do. By the time I am eligible to run for Presidency I will have educated children and adults on the realities of this world, but speaking is not enough, actions are heard through out time.

Being Haitian owned, we have first-hand knowledge on the environment and lifestyles of Haitians in poverty. We stand for a greater purpose which is eliminating poverty in the country that was once the most prosperous in the world. In result to consuming or inhaling cannabis, the main side effect is developing "munchies" a term used to explain suddenly increased appetite. My bakery will focus on giving people the munchies in relations to experiencing how hunger affects Haitians who have nothing to eat at all. I will ask customers to try to postpone eating a meal after gaining the munchies to have empathy for those who starve around the world as a challenge. This will help with my plan of feeding the world to end the pain of hunger

Trafficking Tip Four: Business is business

Business is the primary concern of a trafficker, they need to recruit women to make money. Therefore the more women they lure, the more profit they make. Your trafficker may come to you interested in being your "boyfriend" to soften his presence but as soon as you give him money you are his employee. It is unlikely your trafficker will be romantically interested in you, regardless if you both engage in intercourse. If given the chance to choose between you or another opportunity to make money, they will choose with their best interests. You can be "fired" at any time with no explanation and will not get your money back. Business is done in cash only, because it is untraceable to themselves since it is a crime. Pimps make promises for profit.

Chapter 5 | Canada Eh?

***We are going on vacation;
to CAN-A-DUH!?***

I REMEMBER MY FINAL day in Miami Florida like it was yesterday; my third-grade teacher took away my recesses which made school strictly educational. One day I went to class bright and early and asked if I could go to the library. She told me I would have to be back before the bell rang, I agreed because it happened to be the final day of the annual book fair. We agreed no recess for the rest of the year if I were to come back after the bell. I agreed and made my way down to purchase a book. Indecisive, I changed my mind last minute to choose another book, by the time I got back in line it was packed. The bell rang and two boys came to escort me back to class. My teacher held up to her promise and took away all my recesses and I was stuck sitting out from physical activities, I didn't even get my book. She would even take us outside frequently for the end of the day. Mrs. L loved jeopardy and made it a weekly game for us to play, she offered a rare $2 bill to the student who answered the question correctly. That was the last time I was interested in what she had to say. Fast forward to the last day in the class, I only told one person that I was going on vacation to Canada but to my surprise I was actually moving half way across the world.

    As we got to the airport, I had my snickers and preschool workbooks that my mother had bought me. It was a beautiful sunny day and I remember looking for the outlets to charge her phone. Next thing I know we begin boarding a plane and I was so excited to finally go on vacation. We landed in New York where the weather changed to cold and snowy due to winter. I was shocked that I was looking at snow on TV days prior to actually standing in it. My mother bought me a jacket with a small plastic bag to hold your snow in and I thought where did she get all these clothes from? This was the beginning of my book before I knew it. I left Miami so happy because I was escaping from my book fair bet, with my mother being the hero saving me into a new environment in the beginning of the decade to now. Deciding to leave Canada writing my very own book that could possibly change her life. Who would have known that she was taking me away from my biggest struggles as a little girl only for me to take her away from her struggles as an adult.

Canada is the second largest country in the world with three territories and ten provinces ruled by the Queen. Money is waterproof and smells like maples when you scratch the bank note. Canada is cold with maple trees that is tapped and made into maple syrup that is deliciously poured on your pancakes. Canada is where I lived for most of my life, giving me my biggest wins and my toughest losses in one decade. I was meant to travel to this foreign land next door from the USA for character development, I believe. I have worked so much for other people and the only time I learned valuable lessons is when I worked for myself. If someone asked me where I was from, I would respond with Miami, Florida but I would mention how I went on a thirteen year vacation to Niagara Falls, Ontario, Canada. The best aspect of Niagara Falls is being on Clifton Hill next to the greatest waterfall accessible to man. The waterfall is so powerful you can hear the white noise as-well as see four spotlights hovering the sky at night, accessible to me while camping in my backyard. Clifton Hill has been the heart of Niagara since I was a little girl and will still be here for my own children to experience. Niagara Falls generates electricity for 4.4 million homes, 3 of which I once called home. If I were to spend the rest of my life in the same city I would be the most regular person with a boring life but instead I want to take the risk to make a name for myself. I've been trapped in my story for years only to realize this is not my permanent destination.

One smart move from my mother has created a butterfly effect situation for myself to break the generational poverty in my family. I created a foundation Apples & Sunshine to explain how our existence revolves around the sun as it's UV rays are being absorbed by the melanin of our skin. Brown is the most dominant gene, yet we are the weakest race in the world who constantly have to prove our worth, even if it costs us our lives.

The most predominant malnourished countries are homes of people of colour. How do we allow other people to grow in darkness when the pain of hunger eats them alive? The new meaning of the Apple the "forbidden fruit" is hunger should be forbidden. I have a dream of UNITY in the country which history can change for the greater good. If we all as humans can agree on the aspect of time turning one orbit of the sun into segments by programming your lives around this construct as if it were real then why don't those who starve day and night get any acknowledgment of their pain? Time is ticking each day and there are people who have no access to food. Yawning and a rumbling stomach is our brain's mechanism that signals that we need to eat nutritious food in order to maintain proper bodily function until we sleep to the glowing of the moon. The brain is the most important organ because it is critically in control of homeostasis in the body. When you go long periods of time without food your brain signals your body to quite literally eat itself to gain the nutrients that are stored in your body in order to survive. Two hormones are released in response to hunger which are ghrelin (physical) and leptin (chemical). Before you eat, ghrelin levels increase as leptin levels decrease and vice versa after eating. Imbalance of these hormones result in eating disorders and/or starvation. The heart is the strongest muscle in the body by circulating blood through the blood vessels in the body back to the heart and arteries which carry oxygenated blood away from the heart to the body. Vessels can become narrow through the buildup of plaque made up of cholesterol. Maintaining a healthy lifestyle is the only way to prevent additional build up. As the saying an apple a day keeps the doctor away the nutrients and antioxidants and apples may reduce the risk of diseases coming in the black community. Understanding how our bodies function is essential to life especially since our bodies are constantly elevating. The plateau diet is a regimen believing that humans should eat like our hunter gathering ancestors by consuming meat, fish, vegetables, fruits, and nuts. Due to high poverty rates, 80% of the population in Haiti lives under the poverty line.

A simple exercise will allow you to understand how complex our bodies really are. Grab an apple and take a bite if you do not have an apple nearby, use your imagination. The moment your teeth pierce in, mechanical and chemical digestion have started as juices hit your taste buds and begin to break down the molecules. Continue to chew the Apple until it becomes a mush like baby food product allowing you to swallow by easily passing through the cardiac sphincter where involuntary movement of the esophagus pushes it down to your pyloric sphincter, into your stomach. Fun fact you can swallow solids upside down your esophagus because it contracts in a process called paralysis. Your stomach has both mechanical and chemical digestion where the smooth muscles relax until large volumes of apples are stored in the bottom where muscle contraction begins mixing the bolus together with hydrochloric acid breaking it down. Then your stomach empties its contents into the small intestine which breakdown carbohydrates and proteins. Once the bolus is completely absorbed, all the nutrients travel through the capillaries within the folds of the small intestine covered with microvilli onto the bloodstream. The remaining mush travels to the large intestine with water and leftover nutrients are absorbed such as fiber and digestive pieces travel to your bottom.

Toilette de Anicette will be a bathroom appliance company that supplies toilets and renovated bathrooms to Haitians because there are no sanitary bathrooms available. If any, sanitary bathrooms do not exist to majority of the population because of the lack of up to date appliances out in the nature. The average person needs to have bowel movements at least three times a week. I am aiming towards everyday life to be accessible to everyone, helping small increments of people until I reach, I desired goal. The roaring 20's is my approach to ending world hunger in the aspect of roaring in the tummy in addition to music for the soul. There is an end to every beginning, focusing with every person that ends a meal start to finish onto a global population of people in starved areas, eating.

The underground railroad was a secret passage that saved a total of 30,000 slaves who fled to Canada. Harriet Tubman is one of the most recognized people in Canadian and Black history associated with the Underground railroad. She saved hundreds of slaves to freedom from America to Canada by following the north star. Slaves risked losing everything they had including their very own lives just to attempt to get freedom for themselves and their families.

Even though this was an exceptionally long and dangerous way of traveling especially by foot, it was the safest way to cross boarders because at the time, the railroad was unknown. During the time of the underground railroad, gospel songs were used to serve as secret codes/messages to the slaves. The songs would tell the runaway slaves how to get to freedom. Follow the drinking gourd referred to the big dipper and when the slaves sang "follow the drinking gourd" it was a signal to the runaway slaves to run towards the big dipper (facing the north star) and along the way they would meet with Harriet Tubman or another abolitionist and escape to freedom. Wade in the water told the runaway slaves that the best escape route to freedom was along the river. Slaves also used secret codes of the safest routes disguised as braids in their hair, therefore you should think twice before discriminating against nappy hair follicles. Rice would often be braided into the hair for food for the long journey ahead.

Late at night, these songs could be heard along the cabins of the slaves along the route, guiding the runaways to freedom. Harriet Tubman was Born in Dorchester County, Maryland, United States. Harriet Tubman was one of the most successful conductors of the Underground railroad and is known to be the "Black Moses". She spent her entire childhood working without payment for the benefit of her owners. Preferring the work in the fields, she was able to learn about following geographical directions and about helpful plants from her father and her brothers.

These survival skills came in handy when Tubman later realized that the only way, she could gain her freedom was to run away. Her owner fell ill, putting her in a difficult position; to settle debts, owners would sell their slaves and reduce their holdings. Harriet fled north, making her way to Philadelphia, where she learned about the connections of the Underground Railroad. She sought to free her family and friends and began rescue missions. Initially, she and her charges were safe in the northern US, but with a change in the laws, she had to go to Canada. Harriet Tubman then began and ended her rescues at St. Catharines; and lived there for eight years. Harriet Tubman died on March 10, 1913, in Auburn, New York, United States.

I work best with individuals and unique creativity;

if I can combine those two and make multiple people I come across millionaires; I can create a network of people who can actively change the world. An apple tree planted in representation of my clients will symbolize feeding the world but also generational wealth growing through a family tree. Using Harriet Tubman's blue print I will eventually have a thousand people that I will produce ideas with and turn them into millionaires for themselves or their children. My unique business will bring me the title of saving people as an inspiration by changing people's lives. Many are trapped in the world we live in not belonging to ourselves, working for other people and realize our potential when it is too late or throw it away. It is a personal satisfaction to make entrepreneurs of people that would be stuck working their lives away. Canadian history will help me change history by accomplishing a similar goal for myself and my clients: Freedom.

Trafficking Tip Five: Healing

Healing is the only component in this journey that holds 100% importance to your life. All things come to an end, but healing is constant. Whether it is 3 days or 3 years it does not go away but it gets better if you are honest with your emotions. Denial of what you experienced will quickly have you spiralling to rock bottom which will force you to go up and make it to the top. Healing will give you a sense of super-powers that you never knew were there before. Healing is not always a beautiful journey but the outcome is. You will have to live out the rest of your life if you are able to escape. Most people suppress their emotions because they do not want to believe they let someone get the best of them- but it is a common reality most people struggle with. You do not want to unknowingly hold onto your anger which will effect everyone in your life. Paranoia is the most important aspect of healing, your mind will be scared and want to protect itself, it can dig up fears you never knew existed, brought onto you by the dark energy you were surrounded by. Once you colour over black crayon on white paper it will never turn white again even if you colour over top with a white crayon, the best outcome you will receive will be grey.

The Kissing Booth logo, the first triple meaning business venture of Kimberly C. Anicette

May 22, 2018; Misa Hylton watching Kimberly's story on Instagram before she auditioned for making the Band 2020

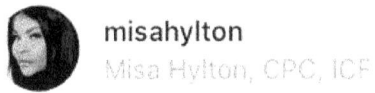

misahylton
Misa Hylton, CPC, ICF

Kimberly's creative inventions on Tik Tok

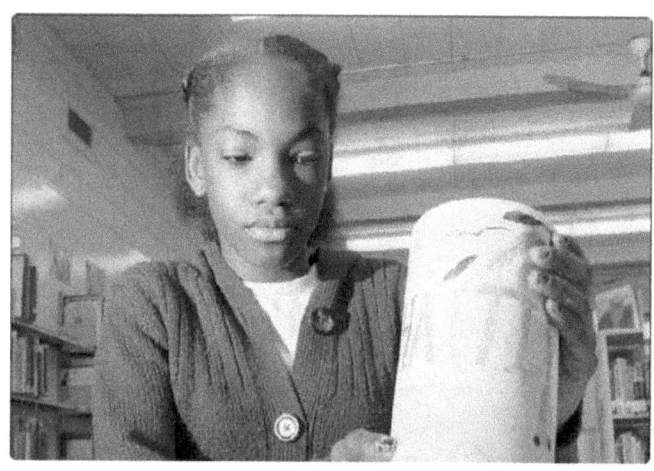

REVIEW NIAGARA FALLS

One small school makes a big effort for Haiti

Proof of the fraudulent actions of the Red Cross building homes in Haiti

Marie Arago, special to ProPublica

How the Red Cross Raised Half a Billion Dollars for Haiti and Built Six Homes

Even as the group has publicly celebrated its work, insider accounts detail a string of failures

by Justin Elliott, ProPublica, and Laura Sullivan, NPR

June 3, 2015

Kimberly holding a jar of donations she designed for Haiti relief fund thanks to her principal Mr. L January 6, 2010

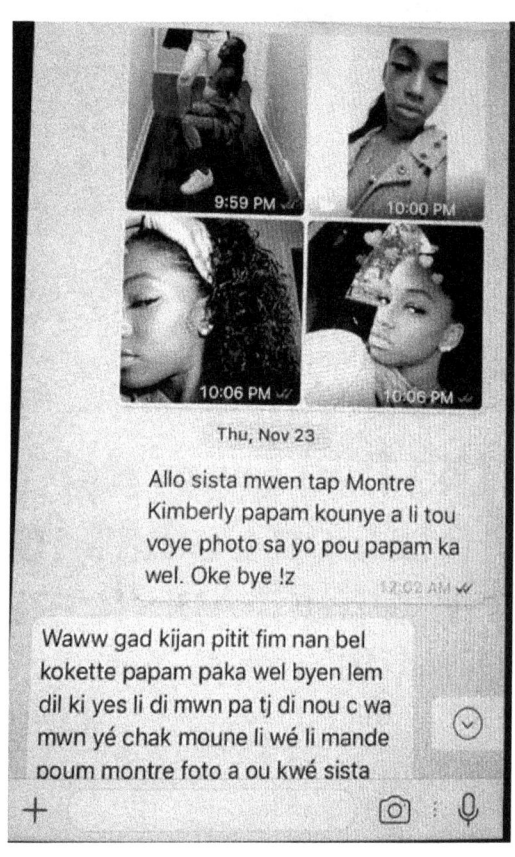

Kimberly sipping her Hi-C juice box while unknowingly signaling her wedding finger standing next to her aunts with blue and white and red stripes resembling the American flag

The last time speaking to my grandfather "The King"

Translation: Woww look at how my granddaughter is beautiful; my father cannot see well he asked who is that and said didn't I tell you I am the King! Every person he sees he asks me to show this picture would you believe it sister? – Andre Felix

November 14th, 2017

IN THIS AUTOBIOGRAPHY of Kimberly C. Anicette, a young girl wearing apple barrettes becomes an advocate for her movement trafficking my apple, representing those sexually exploited for the profit of a pimp. Originally from Miami, Florida, Kimberly's dual citizenship will determine which country she chooses as the 14-year mark to be eligible for the Presidential campaign is approaching.

www.ingramcontent.com/pod-product-compliance
Lightning Source LLC
Chambersburg PA
CBHW051702160426
43209CB00004B/988